EDINBURGH UNIVERSITY PUBLICATIONS

LANGUAGE & LITERATURE No. 6

INTRODUCTION TO THE QUR'ĀN

BY

RICHARD BELL

M.A., D.D.

LATE READER IN ARABIC
UNIVERSITY OF EDINBURGH

EDINBURGH
AT THE UNIVERSITY PRESS

NORTH AMERICAN AGENTS: ALDINE PUBLISHING COMPANY
64 EAST VAN BUREN STREET
CHICAGO 5 ILLINOIS

First Edition 1953
Reprinted 1958, 1963

PRINTED IN GREAT BRITAIN BY
MORRISON & GIBB LTD., LONDON AND EDINBURGH

PREFACE

I HAVE long felt that there is need in English for a general introduction to the Qur'ān, and, as time has been given me, I have attempted to supply it.

This book should, indeed, have accompanied my translation (*The Qur'ān. Translated, with a Critical Rearrangement of the Surahs.* Edinburgh : T. & T. Clark, 1937, 1939). Various reasons, particularly that of health, led me at that time to concentrate on the preparation of the translation as the best way of setting out the results at which I had arrived. The views of Muhammad and of the Qur'ān on which my analysis of the surahs was based have not always been understood, and I have taken this opportunity to make them clearer.

The class lectures from which the book has developed have largely disappeared in the process of revision, though they may still show through, here and there. I am indebted to Professor Emeritus W. B. Stevenson for counsel and encouragement. In spite of his advice, faults of arrangement still remain. There are, no doubt, other defects, but I see no hope of making further improvements. Footnotes have been kept to a minimum. My debt to previous works is sufficiently manifest, especially that to Noeldeke's *Geschichte des Korans*, the second edition of which, revised by Schwally and others, is denoted by N-S. The surahs are denoted by small capital Roman numerals ; the verse numbering is that of Fluegel's edition. The differences between it and the Official Egyptian Edition are shown in the Table which immediately follows the Table of Contents.

I have to thank my wife for constant care and furtherance, and my niece, Mrs. Liddiatt, for relieving me of the labour of typing.

R. B.

PUBLISHERS' NOTE

THIS *Introduction* does not include the 'mass of notes' which, as Dr. Bell stated in the preface to his *Translation*, had to be omitted from that work owing to the cost of printing. These are, in the main, notes on the text of the Qur'ān, and may be published if circumstances permit.

Dr. Bell did not live to read the proofs of this book. At his request they have been read by his friends Mr. Gilbert Watson, C.B.E., formerly H.M. Senior Chief Inspector of Schools in Scotland, and the Rev. A. T. Gordon, M.A., formerly Professor of Arabic and Islamic Studies in the American University, Cairo. Mrs. Bell wishes to express her indebtedness both to them for their labour of love and to Messrs. R. & R. Clark's compositors and readers for the skill with which they have carried out their difficult task.

CONTENTS

TABLE OF DIFFERENCES

BETWEEN THE VERSE-NUMBERS IN FLUEGEL'S EDITION AND THOSE IN THE OFFICIAL EGYPTIAN EDITION

The left-hand column gives Fluegel's numbers : the corresponding numbers in the Egyptian text may be obtained by adding or subtracting as indicated in the right-hand column.

I . . .	1-6	+1
II . . .	1-19	+1
	19-38	+2
	38-61	+3
	61-63	+4
	63-73	+5
	73-137	+6
	138-172	+5
	173-212	+4
	213-216	+3
	217-218	+2
	219-220	+1
	236-258	−1
	259-269	−2
	270-273	−3
	273-274	−2
	274-277	−1
III . . .	1-4	+1
	4-18	+2
	19-27	+1
	27-29	+2
	29-30	+3
	30-31	+4
	31-43	+5
	43-44	+6
	44-68	+7
	69-91	+6
	92-98	+5
	99-122	+4
	122-126	+5
	126-141	+6
	141-145	+7
	146-173	+6
	174-175	+5
	176-179	+4

III *contd.*	180-190	+3
	191-193	+2
	194	+1
	196-198	+1
IV. . . .	3-5	+1
	7-13	−1
	14	−2
	15	−3
	16-29	−4
	30-32	−5
	32-45	−4
	45-47	−3
	47-48	−2
	49-70	−3
	70-100	−2
	100-106	−1
	118-156	+1
	156-170	+2
	171-172	+1
	174-175	+1
V	3-4	−1
	5-8	−2
	9-18	−3
	18-19	−2
	20-35	−3
	35-52	−4
	53-70	−5
	70-82	−4
	82-88	−3
	88-93	−2
	93-98	−1
	101-109	+1
VI. . .	66-72	+1
	136-163	−1
VII . .	1-28	+1

VII *contd.*	28-103	+2
	103-131	+3
	131-139	+4
	140-143	+3
	144-146	+2
	147-157	+1
	166-186	+1
	191-205	+1
VIII . .	37-43	−1
	44-64	−2
	64-76	−1
IX. . .	62-130	−1
X . . .	11-80	−1
XI. . .	6	−1
	7-9	−2
	10-22	−3
	22-54	−2
	55-77	−3
	77-84	−2
	84-87	−1
	88-95	−2
	96-99	−3
	99-120	−2
	120-122	−1
XII . .	97-103	−1
XIII . .	6-18	−1
	28-30	+1
XIV . .	10-11	−1
	12-13	−2
	14-24	−3
	25-26	−4
	27-37	−5
	37	−4
	37-41	−3
	41-42	−2

TABLE OF DIFFERENCES

XIV *contd.*	42-45	−1	XXII *contd.*	26-43	−1	XL *contd.*	33-39	−2
	46-47	−2		43-77	+1		40-56	−3
	47-51	−1	XXIII . .	28-34	−1		56-73	−2
XVI . .	22-24	−1		35-117	−2		73-74	−1
	25-110	−2		117	−1	XLI . .	1-26	+1
	110-128	−1	XXIV . .	14-18	+1	XLII . .	1-11	+2
XVII . .	10-26	−1		44-60	+1		12-31	+1
	27-48	−2	XXV . .	4-20	−1		31-42	+2
	49-53	−3		21-60	−2		43-50	+1
	53-106	−2		60-66	−1	XLIII . .	1-51	+1
	106-108	−1	XXVI . .	1-48	+1	XLIV . .	1-36	+1
XVIII . .	2-21	+1		228	−1	XLV . .	1-36	+1
	23-31	+1	XXVII . .	45-66	−1	XLVI . .	1-34	+1
	31-55	+2		67-95	−2	XLVII . .	5-16	−1
	56-83	+1	XXVIII .	1-22	+1		17-38	−2
	83-84	+2	XXIX . .	1-51	+1	L . . .	13-44	+1
	85-97	+1	XXX . .	1-54	+1	LIII . .	27-58	−1
XIX . . .	1-3	+1	XXXI . .	1-32	+1	LV . .	1-16	+1
	8-14	−1	XXXII . .	1-9	+1	LVI . .	22-46	+1
	27-76	−1	XXXIII .	41-49	+1		66-91	+1
	77-78	−2	XXXIV .	10-53	+1	LVII . .	13-19	+1
	79-91	−3	XXXV .	8-20	−1	LVIII . .	3-21	−1
	91-93	−2		20-21	+1	LXXI . .	5-22	+1
	93-94	−1		21-25	+2		26-29	−1
XX . . .	1-9	+1		25-34	+3	LXXII . .	23-26	−1
	16-34	−1		35-41	+2	LXXIV .	32	−1
	40-41	−1		42-44	+1		33	−2
	42-63	−2	XXXVI .	1-30	+1		34-41	−3
	64-75	−3	XXXVII .	29-47	+1		41-42	−2
	75-79	−2		47-100	+2		42-51	−1
	80-81	−3		101	+1		54-55	+1
	81-88	−2	XXXVIII .	1-43	+1	LXXVIII .	41	−1
	89-90	−3		76-85	−1	LXXX . .	15-18	+1
	90-94	−2	XXXIX .	4	−1	LXXXIX .	1-14	+1
	94-96	−1		5-9	−2		17-25	−1
	106-115	+1		10-14	−3	XCVIII . .	2-7	+1
	115-121	+2		14-19	−2	CI	1-5	+1
	122-123	+1		19-63	−1		5-6	+2
XXI . .	29-67	−1	XL	1-2	+1		6-11	+3
XXII . .	19-21	−1		19-32	−1	CVI . . .	3	+1

CHAPTER I

THE HISTORICAL SITUATION

FEW books have exercised a wider or deeper influence upon the spirit of man than the Qur'ān. By the Moslems, as the followers of Muhammad are properly called, it is regarded as a divine revelation. It is used by them in their public and private devotions, and is recited at their festivals and family occasions. It is the basis of their religious beliefs, their ritual, and their law; the guide of their conduct, both public and private. It moulds their thought, and its phrases enter into their literature and their daily speech. A book thus held in reverence by some three hundred millions of our fellow-men demands our attention. It also demands serious study; for it is by no means an easy book to understand. It is neither a treatise on theology, nor a code of laws, nor a collection of sermons, but rather a medley of all three, with some other things thrown in. It was not written at one time, or according to one scheme, but was delivered from time to time during a period of some twenty years, in the course of which Muhammad, the prophet by whom it was delivered, rose from the position of an obscure religious reformer in his native Meccah to that of virtual ruler of Arabia, in his adopted town of Medinah. As it reflects the changing circumstances, needs and purposes of the Prophet during these years, it naturally varies much in style and content, and even in teaching. Its arrangement is unsystematic, and though it is written in, on the whole, intelligible Arabic, even in its language there are difficulties which scholars have not yet succeeded in explaining.

Before proceeding to study the book itself it will be useful to have before us in brief outline some information as to the historical situation and circumstances of its origin.

THE ENVIRONMENT

The World Situation.—The Qur'ān was produced in the early part of the seventh century A.D. The mission started by Columba was spreading over Scotland and the North of England; that started by St. Austin was spreading over England from the South. The Merovingian kings were nominally reigning in France. The Roman Empire of the West had succumbed to the invasions of the Barbarians. To the Arabs, Rūm meant the Byzantine Empire with its capital at Constantinople. This Eastern Roman Empire, having escaped the ravages which had overtaken the Empire in the West, had attained a position of settled power and civilisation under Justinian, A.D. 527–563, but had thereafter fallen into confusion, partly owing to attacks by other Barbarians from without, and partly because of internal troubles and incapable rulers.

The Persian Empire of the Sassanids had long been the rival of Byzantium in the East. It included Iraq and Mesopotamia; indeed its capital had been fixed at Medā'in Ctesiphon, which lay a few miles south of where the later city of Baghdad now stands. It thus bordered upon the North East of Arabia, just as the Byzantine province of Syria bordered upon the North West. Hostilities were endemic along the frontier of the two empires, and periodically broke out into regular wars. Even the fifty years' peace agreed on towards the end of the reign of Justinian had not been kept, and a long and final struggle began in A.D. 602. Taking advantage of the weakness of Byzantium, Khosrau II of Persia declared war, alleging as his pretext revenge for the murder of the Emperor Maurice, to whose aid he had in the beginning of his reign been indebted. Phocas, who had displaced Maurice, beset by apathy and active revolt at home, was in no position to ward off the Persian attack, and Asia Minor was overrun. The fortunes of Byzantium were at their lowest ebb when in 610 Heraclius, son of the governor of North Africa, appeared with a fleet before Constantinople. Phocas was deposed and Heraclius crowned emperor. But the European provinces of the Empire had also been overrun by Barbarians from the North, and years passed before he was able to make headway against the Persians. Turning southwards, they conquered Syria and Egypt in 614. But the sack of Jerusalem, which had revolted against the Persian garrison, the slaughter of Christians, and the carrying off of what was believed to be the true Cross, stirred the emotions of Christians throughout the Empire. This enabled Heraclius to organise his forces for a determined effort. He had, however, first to deal with the Avars who threatened Constantinople from the North, and it was not till 622 that he was able to turn against the Persians. Thereafter, in campaign after campaign he compelled them to withdraw from Asia Minor, Egypt, and Syria, by using his sea-power to attack them in the rear and to invade their home-provinces. In 627 Khosrau's palace was captured and sacked; he had to flee from his capital, and met his death either from the violence of his own passions or from that of his courtiers. In 628 peace was made, and amongst other conditions was the return of the Cross, which Heraclius the victor restored to Jerusalem.

Arabia.—This contest for world power, which was going on while Muhammad was pursuing his mission in Meccah and Medinah, probably affected Arabia but little. Arabs may have fought in the armies of both empires. It is possible that the disturbed state of the countries to the north of Arabia tended to divert some of the trade between East and West, which would otherwise have passed through them, to the southern route, and may thus have increased the trade of South Arabia and of the Meccan caravans which formed one of the links between South Arabia and the Mediterranean. There may be one or two references to the war in the Qur'ān, though what is usually regarded as a prophecy of Byzantine victory, XXX, 1-4, is perhaps to be interpreted otherwise. But the scene of the fighting was, for the most part, remote from Arabia.

This great peninsula, so largely desert, was in fact protected by the nature of its terrain from warlike invasion from without. The two great powers had been content to maintain on its frontiers something of the nature of buffer-states. The Persians supported the Lakhmid dynasty of Ḥīrah in the North East, while in the North West the Byzantines subsidised the chiefs of the house of Ghassān. In return for this support, these Arab rulers held the raiding Bedouin in check, and maintained the prestige of their respective superiors. Only in the South West had there been any real political penetration. This fertile corner of Arabia had been the seat of an ancient civilisation. But the Sabaeans who latterly had ruled there, had, for some reason, lost their power and their monopoly of trade, see XXXIV, 14 ff. Christianity had been introduced fairly early, and there are traditions of persecutions of the Christians, notably that under the Jewish king, Dhū Nuwās. This led to the invasion of the Yemen by the Abyssinians, and the establishment of an Abyssinian dynasty. Later, just about the time of Muhammad, this had been replaced by Persian rule.

The greater part of Arabia, however, was then, as it still is, a land of nomad tribes. Here and there, where water happened to be found, an oasis gave opportunity for the practice of some primitive agriculture, and especially for the cultivation of palms. The most important of these oases in West Arabia was Yathrib or, as it came to be better known, Medinah. It lay on a fertile plateau, towards the head of the Wadi Hamd, about 130 miles inland from the Red Sea coast, between the 24th and 25th degrees of latitude. Farther north were Khaibar, Taimā', and Dūmah. In these and other places a small settled population was found. Meccah, the largest town of all, owed its population to trade rather than to agriculture, for the surrounding country is sterile. So far as they were Arabs, the inhabitants of the towns and villages do not seem to have differed much from the Bedouin. The same tribal system seems to have prevailed.

The Bedouin.—The Bedouin were intensely proud, boasting their freedom, their prowess in war, their hospitality and their purity of race. They were inclined to despise those who had settled down to agriculture. They all, however, recognised each other as Arabs, and this unity was fostered not only by a sense of race kinship, but by a common language, spoken, no doubt, in many dialects, and by a common heritage of poetry which maintained a standard of the language understood and admired all over the peninsula. But this vague unity of race and tongue was broken by tribal jealousies and feuds. The tribe was the main unit, divided into clans and families, but held together by the council of its leading men. Amongst these, one was usually recognised as chief, but this office, though it might tend to remain in one family, was not hereditary. The holding of it, in fact, depended on ability to take the lead in council and in war. Each tribe had its recognised district, in which it moved as the exigencies of water and pasturage demanded. These varied from season to season, and probably from year to year. The desert character of Arabia is for the most part due, not to the nature of its soil, but to the scantiness and uncertainty of its rainfall. Rain in Arabia is one of the greatest of blessings, and with its coming the face of the desert is transformed. In good seasons life might be pleasant enough, but times were often hard, and famine years not uncommon. Within the tribe a certain brotherhood prevailed, and the chiefs had a sense of responsibility towards the poorer members. In a mercantile town like Meccah, we may surmise, this responsibility sat but lightly on the wealthy. Beyond the limits of the tribe, however, little sense of brotherhood existed. In times of stress weak tribes were bound to suffer, and might be driven from part, or even from the whole, of their domain. The many migrations of which one hears were no doubt due to something of that sort ; though the fact that so-called Southern Arab tribes were found in Central and North Arabia is generally associated with the bursting of the dam of Ma'rib in the Yemen in A.D. 451, an event for which there is historical evidence.

The basis of the tribe was no doubt kinship, though there was more mixture of blood than the theory of the Arab genealogists implies. Outside his own tribe the individual had no rights, and counted for little. But he might be received into the protection of another tribe or of some influential member of it, and so find security. Or he might even be accepted into the tribe as a *ḥalīf*, by a sort of blood-brotherhood constituted by oath. It was probably in some such way that Muhammad's followers at first found a footing in Medinah.

Arab Life and Custom.—The possessions of a tribe consisted of cattle, sheep, and goats, but especially of camels. Horses were much prized, but were delicate animals in desert conditions; only the wealthy could maintain them, and their use was mainly for raids and fighting. It was on his camels that the Badawī mainly depended. He was largely occupied in breeding and rearing them, and from them came most of his simple necessities. Wild animals of the desert offered good hunting at times to those who could afford to take part in it.

Warlike raids were frequent. These for the most part aimed at the capture of booty rather than at bloodshed. But it was a rough game, in which the attempt to drive off cattle and other booty often led to fighting and bloodshed. The law of retaliation prevailed, and, while from one point of view this operated to make the shedding of blood a serious matter which should if possible be avoided, on the other hand, if once blood were shed, an ever-widening feud might develop which would make life unsafe for members of both the tribes involved, and might grow to open warfare. Wiser counsels, however, sometimes prevailed, and a composition was made by balancing up the slain and making a payment of camels. Even then, personal feelings might not be satisfied, and private revenge taken for a near relative might reopen the feud.

Position of Women.—In such a state of society the position of women must have been insecure. The strength of a tribe lay in its fighting men. The birth of a son was welcomed, that of a daughter was often felt as a disappointment. To what extent the custom prevailed of burying female children alive is difficult to discover. The Qur'ān affords evidence that it sometimes happened, VI, 138, XVI, 61, LXXXI, 8 f. That it prevailed extensively is hardly likely. For, in a sense, daughters were valuable property. Marriage was by purchase, the *mahr* or bride-price being paid to the parent or guardian. Women were also frequently carried off in raids, becoming the wives of their captors. This implies that women were regarded as property. We are told that they might be inherited as part of the property of a deceased husband, though it is doubtful if this is referred to in IV, 23. The fact that a husband claimed rights of possession in a wife did not necessarily prevent the wife having property of her own, nor did it altogether prevent women from exercising some amount of influence. They seem to have enjoyed considerable freedom and respect. But they had few rights. Divorce was common, and at the will of the man, though a woman's kinsmen might have influence enough to prevent too great injustice being done. The migrations of nomad life no doubt tended to induce temporary relationships, and when women were carried off in raids little regard was paid to the marriage bond.

Sacred Months.—The uncertainty of this state of raiding and war, which seems to have been almost normal in Arabia, was to some extent mitigated by the institution of sacred months. Of these there were four in the year, Rajab, standing by itself, the other three, Dhū l-Qaʿdah, Dhū l-Ḥijjah and Muḥarram, forming a group at the end and beginning of the Arab year. In the middle of this period the Meccan pilgrimage was held annually. In these months, by long-established custom, war and fighting were forbidden, and in spite of the lawlessness of Arab life the prohibition seems on the whole to have been observed. The Arab months were lunar, but the year was kept in line with the seasons by the insertion of an extra month occasionally. When this should be done was, in all probability, decided at Meccah during the pilgrimage time.

Meccah.—Meccah had at this time become the leading town of Arabia. It was dependent on its trade. Its possession of a well had made it a halting-place on the trade route which ran north and south roughly parallel to the Red Sea, and also on that which ran from the interior of Arabia to the Red Sea coast. The town had grown to be of much importance. The North-South route was one of the arteries of trade between East and West, and the trade passing along it, which had at one time been in the hands of the

Sabaeans, and later shared by them with the Nabataeans, seems now to have fallen into the hands of the Meccans. Meccah had thus become a place of wealth, business and political influence. It was, in addition, a religious centre, for it possessed a famous sanctuary, the Ka'bah, and was surrounded by a *ḥaram*, or sacred territory, in which by religious sanction fighting and bloodshed were forbidden. The annual pilgrimage, which seems in pagan times to have been connected with other sanctuaries in the neighbourhood of Meccah rather than with the Ka'bah, drew together tribesmen from all over Arabia. Under shelter of the sacred months fairs were held at various places in the neighbourhood, and no doubt a good deal of secular and political business was transacted. The frequency with which the Qur'ān insists that it is impossible to frustrate Allah probably combats the confidence the Meccans had in their powers of negotiation and intrigue to avert threatening dangers.

Religion.—Religion, it will be seen, still exercised much influence in Arabia. But this was probably due more to respect for ancient custom than to the strength of active belief in the pagan gods. These gods, of whom we really know little beyond the names, seem to have been connected partly with worship of the heavenly bodies (al-'Uzzā is probably the planet Venus, and al-Lāt a name for the sun-goddess), partly with a worship of fate or destiny (al-Manāt has probably some such sense), and partly with a more primitive animism. They were associated with particular places, and seem to have been represented by rough stone-images, or perhaps simply by stones of some peculiar shape which had acquired a reputation of sanctity. Sacrifices were offered to the gods, usually camels, sheep or goats. There are hints of human sacrifices having occasionally taken place, but these were certainly not characteristic of Arabian religion. The exposure of female infants may have had a religious basis, but was more probably due to economic causes. The Qur'ān mentions some food-taboos, no doubt connected with the sacrifices. Pilgrimages were made to sanctuaries, and the circumambulation of them seems to have been a common practice. We know most about the pilgrimage of Meccah, and the circumambulation of the Kaʿbah, which with some modifications were ultimately adopted into Islam, and still continue. But these, though the most important of such ceremonies, were not the only ones in Arabia.

Jinn.—In ordinary life, belief in demons and jinn was probably more alive in the mind of the Arab than belief in the gods. These shadowy spirits seldom assumed a distinct personality or a name. They were associated with deserts, ruins and other eerie places, and might assume various forms, usually those of animals, serpents and other creeping things. Though vaguely feared, they were not always inimical. A madman was *majnūn*, that is, affected by the jinn, but the jinn were sometimes also thought of as assisting men to special knowledge. That the poet was at one time thought of as having some such demonic inspiration is implied in the name *shāʿir* 'one who is aware' or 'perceives'. The position of the *kāhin* 'soothsayer' is by no means clear. He appears not to have been specially attached to any sanctuary, or to the service of a particular god, but to have had his own special prompter, a spirit or jinn, who inspired him, and to have carried on his operations independently. Arab legend has much to tell of these men—women occasionally pretended to such inspiration—and though in detail entirely untrustworthy, it no doubt conveys a true enough picture of the customs which prevailed. They were consulted on all sorts of matters, for prognostications of the future, for the solution of past mysteries, and for decisions on litigious questions. Their oracles were often cryptic, garnished with oaths to make them more impressive, and usually couched in *sajʿ* 'rhymed prose', short rhythmic lines rhyming with each other. It is probable that the existence of such a class of men, and the style of their oracles, had some influence upon Muhammad, though he denied that he was a *kāhin*.

Judaism.—We have also, however, as a mere glance at the Qur'ān will show, to reckon with the influence of the higher religions of Judaism and Christianity. Judaism had been known in Arabia for at least several centuries. In the Yemen, the Jews had at one time taken a leading position, and no doubt were still represented by a strong colony in the Prophet's day. In practically all the oases of the North West of the peninsula we hear of settlements of Jews, in Taimā', Fadak, Wadi l-Qurā, Khaibar, and especially in Yathrib (Medinah). They seem to have been agriculturalists rather than traders, and, curiously enough, the evidence of their presence in the trading centre, Meccah, is rather uncertain. On the ground of the names which are mentioned in Tradition, and of the fact that they seem to have been divided into tribes and clans, it has been argued that these settlers were not Jews by race, but were Arabs who had adopted the Jewish religion. But, though there may have been Arab proselytes among them, it seems impossible to understand the part which these people play in the life of Muhammad without assuming that there was at least a strong kernel of Jewish race. As they appear in the Qur'ān, they have the characteristics of the Jew.

Christianity.—Christianity prevailed in most of the countries lying round about Arabia. It was the official religion of the Byzantine Empire. The Melkite, or Orthodox State Church, was, however, not popular in the provinces bordering on Arabia. The Chalcedonian formula of the two natures, divine and human, in the one person of Jesus Christ, had been adopted in A.D. 451. But the dispute had continued, and had led to the formation of separate Churches. In Syria the Jacobite Church was strong, and held to its Monophysite doctrine, laying emphasis on the divine nature of Jesus Christ. The Coptic Church in Egypt was also Monophysite, as was the Church in Abyssinia. In the Yemen, where Christianity had found a footing some centuries before, the Church was influenced by the Abyssinian Church, and was, like it, Monophysite.

Zoroastrianism.—The official religion of the Persian Empire was Zoroastrianism, with its dualism of light and darkness, good and evil. The existence at least of this religion was known to Muhammad, for its adherents are referred to under the name *al-majūs* in XXII, 17. It is therefore possible that he may have borrowed from it, but the fact that in other similar lists, II, 59, V, 73, *al-majūs* does not occur, suggests that his knowledge of it was remote and came late. In fact the buffer state of Ḥīrah, through which the Persian Empire came more immediately into contact with Arabia, was largely Christian in population. There was a strong body of Christians there and in the confines of the Persian Empire itself. This Church, somewhat isolated from the main body of Christendom, had maintained the older type of Christian doctrine associated with the name of Nestorius, and, on the whole, stressed the human nature of Jesus Christ. Sometimes repressed, but more usually enjoying an uneasy toleration, it was an active missionary Church, and spread the knowledge of Christianity far into the interior of Asia, and also amongst the Arab tribes.

Religious Penetration.—The extent to which Christianity had really penetrated into Arabia is difficult to gauge. Certain tribes, especially in the North East, were nominally Christian. A flourishing Hellenic-Christian civilisation is attested in the district east of the Jordan and the Dead Sea. We hear of Christians among the settled population of some of the oases of the North West of the peninsula, particularly in Dūmah and Taimā', and there was a bishop in Ailah at the head of the Gulf of 'Aqabah. But as to the centre of the peninsula, we are in the dark. Many of the Arab poets make reference to Christian objects and customs. This is natural, as it was part of the policy of the kings of Ḥīrah and of the chiefs of Ghassān to encourage Arab poets to visit their courts. But the knowledge implied in these references is limited to externals and seldom goes beyond what an observant visitor might acquire. On the other hand, the nature of Arabic poetry did not allow the expression of any deeper understanding of religion, and there may have been more behind these casual references than appears. All we can say is that there is no evidence of the spirit of Arab poetry having been modified by Christian ideas. But certainly, through visitors, and especially by the coming and going of merchants and traders, it was possible for enquiring spirits in Arabia to acquire a knowledge of Christianity. There may even have been wandering missionaries of that faith appearing at Arab gatherings, as Tradition affirms

Tradition also speaks of certain Arabs who about Muhammad's time had turned away from paganism ; some inclined to Christianity, among them Waraqah b. Nawfal, a cousin of Muhammad's wife Khadījah, who is said to have studied the books of the Christians. Western scholars have always been suspicious of the details of these traditions, but have been inclined to accept the fact of the existence of these *ḥanīfs* as evidence of the influence of Judaism and Christianity upon the Arabs. Unfortunately they belong to the development of Muhammad's thought rather than to history.

The word *ḥanīf* occurs several times in the Qur'ān, evidently in the sense of one who follows a pure religion, ' not a polytheist '. The derivation of the word has been much discussed. The Arabs derive it from the root *ḥnf* which means ' to incline ', ' lean to one side ' ; hence the word would mean ' one who leans away from the prevailing religion '. But the use of the word in the Qur'ān implies a much more positive sense. Western scholars have been inclined to connect it with the Syriac *ḥanpā*, 'heathen'. This suits the use of the word in Arabic poetry before Muhammad's time, where it occurs a few times. But it does not suit the Qur'ān usage. The further difficulty of the long vowel in the second syllable of *ḥanīf* is resolved if we suppose the word to have been borrowed first in its plural form ; Syriac *ḥanĕphē* would readily give *ḥunafā'* in Arabic, and this would imply *ḥanīf* as its singular. This gives us a hint as to how the word came into Arabic, for in Syriac speech the Arabs were, religiously, *ḥanĕphē*, that is, heathen. They were polytheists, but Muhammad, in the course of his controversy with the Jews and Christians, came to the conclusion that religions were apt to be corrupted from their pristine purity. As the Jews and Christians of his day were the degenerate representatives of original pure monotheisms established by Moses and Jesus, so the *ḥunafā'* were the degenerate representatives of an original pure religion established by Abraham. Abraham, therefore, the founder of this Arab religion, was, as is repeatedly stated in the Qur'ān, a " *ḥanīf*, but not a polytheist ". Thus *ḥanīf* acquired in the Qur'ān the sense of pure monotheist. In so far as the tradition shows the influence of this change of sense, it is dependent on the Qur'ān.

Jewish-Christian Sects.—Whether, for the explanation of the Qur'ān, we require to take account of some heretical form, or forms, of Christianity is a debatable point. The mixture of Jewish and Christian material which it contains has raised the question whether we have not to assume that Muhammad had been in contact with some Jewish-Christian sect. And it is, of course, possible that some such forms of Christianity may have lingered along the borders of Arabia long after they had died out elsewhere.

In this connection attention has been called to the Elkesaites, a Jewish-Christian (perhaps originally Jewish) sect mentioned by Eusebius and also by Hippolytus. It seems to have been founded by Elkesai, who professed to have received a Book sent down to him from Heaven, *c.* A.D. 100. They rejected sacrifices, and stressed the practice of baptism, in the form of total immersion, for the remission of sins. In prayer they turned towards Jerusalem, and they insisted on the observance of the Sabbath. They disliked the teaching of Paul, denied the Virgin Birth, and practised a form of sacrament in bread and salt. That they are said to have been vegetarians may simply mean that they refused to eat flesh which had been offered in sacrifice.

Mention may also be made of the Mandaeans, who were later identified with the Ṣābi'īn mentioned in the Qur'ān, though this identification is by no means certain. They were a syncretistic sect, probably of pagan origin, living in the region of the lower Euphrates, where remnants of them are still to be found. The most notable element of their ritual was immersion in running water. Their belief showed admixture of Jewish, Gnostic, and Christian elements. Their adoption of John the Baptist as their chief saint probably dates from after the Moslem conquest, and it is unlikely that they had any historical connection with him.

Another system from which some have thought that Muhammad may have borrowed is Manichaeism. Its origin is obscure, but it seems to have arisen from the teaching of Mānī (or Mānich), who was born in Babylonia *c.* A.D. 216, and *c.* A.D. 242 began to claim that he had received divine messages and to carry on a religious mission. He seems to have claimed to be one of a succession of divine messengers, Buddha, Zoroaster, Jesus. But what place in his system was assigned to these predecessors is not clear. Manichaeism claimed to be a philosophy and an ethical system based upon revelation. Its philosophy makes much of the imaginative contrast between light and darkness, good and evil, spirit and matter, though it is not clear how far it actually identified evil with matter, or in fact what its conception of matter really was. Its ethical code was, however, somewhat whimsically ascetic, and fasting played a large part in it. The movement spread first in the Persian Empire, where it met with persecution. It was thus driven into Central Asia. Its spread in the West dates from about the fourth century. There it appealed strongly to the intelligentsia, and for a time was amongst them a serious rival to Christianity.

We cannot *a priori* rule out the possibility that any of these sects may have exercised some influence upon Muhammad or his surroundings. To the enquiring Arab mind any idea current in the spiritual atmosphere of surrounding countries might be accessible. Yet on the whole Arabia was remote and primitive, and Muhammad was, after all, a practical man who had spent the early part of his life in business, if not in more menial labour. It will be well therefore to keep as far as possible to the main stream of ideas that were likely to be known to ordinary people, and not allow ourselves to be lured aside by every attractive similarity which scholarship may reveal.

Cultural Penetration.—Some of the things which Arabia needed it could no doubt procure. But its wants were limited by its remoteness, its restricted resources and its primitive mode of life. Swords and lances appear to have been common enough, though they no doubt came mostly from outside. The protective ring-mail, which came from Persia, could be procured only by the chiefs. Wine, the product of the grape, was imported by Jewish or Christian merchants, but the very frequency with which poets boast of having drunk it shows that it was not an ordinary beverage.

Writing.—The question which interests us here is the prevalence of writing. The assumption which at one time prevailed that writing in Muhammad's day was a recent introduction into Arabia, known only to a few and still regarded as a marvel, has been disproved. It rested to some extent on a misinterpretation of XCVI, 4, which was taken as ascribing the teaching of the use of the pen to Allah as one of His outstanding gifts to men. The real sense is that Allah had taught by means of the pen, that is, had given a written revelation of things which men could not otherwise know That writing was known in Arabia long before that time is shown by archaeological evidence. There are South Arabian inscriptions going back, some of them, far beyond the Christian era. In North West Arabia inscriptions have been found, in various alphabets, Nabataean, Liḥyānic, Thamūdic, which belong to the centuries preceding the appearance of Muhammad. The Arabic alphabet is sparsely attested: there is one inscription dating from A.D. 328, and there are two belonging to the sixth century. That is no doubt meagre enough. Still we may assume that, where inscriptions on stone or metal occur, writing on some more convenient material was already fairly well known. In fact, anyone who considers the relationship of these various alphabets to each other will recognise that the development is one of written forms, which tend to grow more cursive, and therefore less suitable for inscriptional use. This implies a pretty active use of writing. True, no inscriptions have yet been found in the neighbourhood of Meccah or Medinah. But Meccah was a mercantile town dependent for its very existence on its trade, and in regular communication with regions in which writing was in common use. The Meccan merchants must have kept some record of their transactions, and it may be assumed that writing was well enough known there. The indirect evidence of the Qur'ān shows that it was. Its imagery is steeped in a mercantile atmosphere, and implies the keeping of accounts in writing. The Judgment-day is the day of reckoning, the books will be opened, and every one will be shown his account, or will get his account handed to him to read. The angels write the deeds of men, and everything is recorded in a book. Some of these images may be borrowed from Christian language; but, even so, they must have been quite well understood in Meccah. The fact that the Qur'ān lays it down that debts should be recorded in writing, II, 282 f., shows that persons able to write were not difficult to find even in Medinah where this regulation was produced.

The tradition as to the collection of the Qur'ān mentions palm-leaves, leather, ribs and shoulder-blades of animals as materials on which portions of the Qur'ān were found to have been written. Possibly the intention behind this is to give an impression of the primitive conditions amid which the Qur'ān originated, and thus heighten the wonder of it. No doubt these things were occasionally used for writing on. But there is no reason why papyrus should not have been used in Meccah at any rate. For purposes of book-production papyrus had by this time given place, in the Graeco-Roman world, to pergament (parchment), which was prepared from the skins of animals, afforded a better surface, and was more enduring. This is perhaps once mentioned in the Qur'ān, LII, 3, by the word *raqq* ; the reference is probably to the Jewish Law given at Sinai. (It may imply that the Jews used pergament for the writing of their Torah.) But papyrus continued to be produced, and was largely used for business purposes and private correspondence. It was made in rectangular sheets of moderate size. In former times, rolls were produced for the writing of books by pasting a number of such sheets together. That had gone out of fashion, but to a certain limited extent the sheets might still be pasted together, or might be folded into book-form. Probably it is this material which is denoted by the word *qirṭās*, which occurs twice in the Qur'ān, VI, 7, 91, for it is derived from the Greek *chartēs* which denotes a leaf or sheet of papyrus. Since it is an early borrowing, and probably not direct from the Greek, there is of course the possibility that it may have undergone some change of meaning, but this is unlikely, as it appears to have still had the signification of papyrus in the days of the caliphs ; (see Mingana, *Woodbrooke Studies*, II, p. 21). VI, 91 may then imply that the Jews used papyrus for writing out separate portions of the Torah ; and VI, 7 shows that the idea of producing a book on papyrus did at least enter Muhammad's mind. What material was denoted by *ṣuḥuf*, we have no means of knowing. The word occurs several times in the Qur'ān, usually in connection with the revelation, XX, 133, LIII, 37, LXXX, 13, LXXXVII, 18 f., XCVIII, 2 ; in LXXIV, 52 and LXXXI, 10, however, it probably refers to the record of man's deeds. The word is South Arabian, but occurs in Arabic poetry before Muhammad's time (see Jeffery, *The Foreign Vocabulary of the Qur'ān*). The singular *ṣaḥīfah* probably denotes a sheet of writing material, so that it would not specify any particular material. The plural *ṣuḥuf* one would naturally take to mean separate (unbound) sheets. It may be argued that when the Qur'ān speaks of the *ṣuḥuf* of Moses or of Abraham something of the nature of a book is implied. But that is not necessarily so. If Muhammad were working with sheets, he would naturally assume that other messengers did the same.

Could Muhammad Write?—The question then arises whether Muhammad used writing materials, and had acquired the art of writing. It has become almost a dogma with Moslems that the Prophet was unable either to read or to write. It enhances the miracle of the Qur'ān that it should have been delivered by one entirely unlettered. Early opinion was not quite so fixed, though on the whole it tended to the same side. One of the main arguments for it is the application of the adjective *ummīy* to the Prophet in the Qur'ān, VII, 156, 158, the word being interpreted to mean 'uneducated'. Properly the word means 'belonging to the *ummah*, the community', and in all the passages where it occurs it is at least possible to translate it 'native', that is, belonging to the Arab community. In the passages where it is applied to the Prophet, this gives perfectly good sense. It was in fact part of his claim that he was an Arab messenger to the Arab people. In some of the passages where the word is used in the plural, see II, 73, III, 69, it might be argued that some contrast is implied between those who knew the Scriptures and those who did not, and it is possible that the Jewish use of the phrase *'ām hā'āreṣ*, in the sense of common, unlettered people may have influenced the meaning. Even if that be so, the use of *ummīy* as applied to the Prophet would imply no more than that he was not familiar with the Jewish (or Christian) Scriptures. Similar is the sense of XXIX, 47: "Thou hast not been in the habit of reciting or tracing with thy hand any book before it; in that case those who invalidate [thy claims] would have been suspicious". That simply means that he had not been a reader or a writer of previous Scriptures, that is, had not been a priest or a scribe; else his opponents might justifiably have been suspicious that he was merely repeating what he had learned from them. These Qur'ān statements then do not necessarily imply that Muhammad could not read or write.

The evidence from Tradition is inconclusive. No great stress can be laid on the Prophet's answer to the angel as reported in the story of his Call, when he was presented with a scroll and told to read (or recite). For, while the words most probably mean " I am not a reader ", that is, " I am unable to read ", they might mean simply " I am not going to read " ; and, as we shall see, the tradition is, as a whole, unreliable. Tradition quite frequently says that Muhammad " wrote ", but as a rule this means no more than that he gave instructions for a written message to be sent. We know that, at any rate in his later years, he employed secretaries. There is in fact a curious story of his employing one of them to write the Qur'ān.[1] Muhammad was dictating to ʿAbdallah b. Saʿd b. Abī Sarḥ the passage XXIII, 12 ff., and when he reached the end of v. 14, he paused, and ʿAbdallah interjected : " Blessed be Allah, the best of creators ". This Muhammad adopted as the needed rhyme-phrase, and told him to write it down. This aroused ʿAbdallah's doubts ; later he gave up Islam and returned to Meccah. He was one of the few proscribed at the time of the conquest, but was pardoned on the intercession of ʿOthman.[2] That does not look like an invented story, and it supports the assumption that Muhammad did keep a written record of his revelations. As to his having written with his own hand, practically the only definite statement to that effect occurs in some of the accounts of what happened at Ḥudaibiyah. It is sometimes said that when the Quraish emissary objected to the designation " Messenger of God " in the heading of the treaty, Muhammad told ʿAlī, who was acting as secretary, to delete it and write " b. ʿAbdallah " instead. ʿAlī refused to delete the title, whereupon Muhammad took the document and deleted it. Some forms of the story say further that he wrote in the altered designation with his own hand. One suspects some ʿAlīite influence in this story of ʿAlī's refusal to delete the title. Other forms of the story, while recording the objection and the dropping of the title—it is really indirectly confirmed in XLVIII, 29—seem to imply that objection was raised before the title was actually written, and are

[1] See Baiḍāwī on VI, 93.

[2] Ibn Hishām, p. 818 ff.

silent about any change being made in the actual document. The evidence of Muhammad having written anything on this occasion is thus very weak.[1] A stronger argument, though indirect, can perhaps be drawn from the story of the sending out of ʿAbdallah b. Jaḥsh on the expedition which led to the attack on the Meccan caravan at Nakhlah on the last day of the sacred month of Rajab of the year II. Muhammad is said to have written a letter of instructions, which he gave to ʿAbdallah, forbidding him to open it until he was two days' march from Medinah.[2] This of course may not mean that he wrote the letter with his own hand. But it is not certain that at this early stage of his career in Medinah he employed secretaries, and the secrecy with which the expedition was despatched makes it doubtful whether he would entrust anyone with the writing of the letter.

There is thus no convincing proof that Muhammad could write. But there is no improbability in his being able to do so. He may quite well have learned the art in Meccah, and if, as Tradition says, he conducted business for Khadījah in his youth, he must surely have been able to keep accounts in some form. The Meccan gibe reported in the Qur'ān, xxv, 6, "Tales of the ancients, which he has written for himself; they are recited to him morning and evening", though it may possibly mean "has had written for himself", shows that at least his critics thought he was working with written material of some sort. His retort in v. 7 does not in direct terms deny that he was doing so. Again, when his opponents gibed at him about the verbosity of Allah, he retorted, xviii, 109: "Were the sea ink for the words of my Lord, the sea would fail before the words of my Lord would fail, though we brought as much ink again"; or as in xxxi, 26: "Were the trees that are in the earth pens, and the sea ink, with seven seas after it to swell it, the words of Allah

[1] The full story is given in Ibn Hishām, p. 747, where ʿAlī is named as the writer. Bukhārī, 54, 15, gives much the same account, but simply says that Muhammad called for a "writer"; 53, 6a, ʿAlī refused to delete "Messenger of God", Muhammad deleted it himself; 53, 6b, adds that he wrote "son of ʿAbdallah" instead; so also 64, 43, which adds that he was not good at writing; 58, 19, expressly says he was unable to write, but made the deletion when ʿAlī refused.

[2] Ibn Hishām, p. 423.

would not give out ". It seems probable that one who made such retorts was using pen and ink. At any rate, should study of the Qur'ān require the assumption that he was doing so, there can be no objection to it on the ground of improbability.

The Value of Tradition.—Study of the Qur'ān must, in fact, be decisive in all questions regarding Muhammad. Tradition with regard to his life, his sayings and doings is profuse. With it there mingles a great deal of pious legend, and it is by no means easy to distinguish what is historical from what was invented for various purposes, or for no purpose but the play of fancy, in the century or two following upon his death. It is necessary therefore to emphasise that for the whole history of Muhammad the Qur'ān must be regarded as the primary source. This is especially true of the early part of his life. In his native town Muhammad was not a person of great importance. In the later years of his residence there he did attract some attention, but there were hardly any outstanding events to impress the popular memory. Historical tradition for that period of his life was therefore scanty, and pious imagination had a very free course. For the last ten years of his life the case is different. During that time he was much in the public eye, and was the centre of memorable events. Concerning these there is a sound historical tradition which enables us to fix the outline of his life and to interpret many passages of the Qur'ān. Even here, however, the principle holds that the Qur'ān is the fundamental authority, and while Tradition may often throw light on the Qur'ān, we can only use Tradition in so far as it is consistent with the Qur'ān, or at any rate is not inconsistent with the Qur'ān properly understood.

MUHAMMAD'S CAREER

All intimate questions regarding the Prophet's personality, his inspiration, claims and purposes, can be answered only on the basis of study of the Qur'ān. But the Qur'ān is so closely related to the life of Muhammad that in approaching it we must have in our minds at least an outline of his career.

Muhammad was born in Meccah. The exact date is uncertain, but is usually reckoned to have been A.D. 570 or 571. His father is said to have died before he was born, and his mother when he was about six years old. The Qur'ān confirms that he was an orphan, that he was brought up in the pagan religion, and began life in poverty; see XCIII, 6-8, which there seems to be no reason for taking otherwise than literally. He was protected by his grandfather 'Abd al-Muṭṭalib, and later by an uncle Abū Ṭālib. With the latter he is said to have accompanied the trading caravan to Syria. No credence can be given to the stories of his contact with Christian monks at this stage. But there are indications in the Qur'ān that the route taken by the caravans to the North was not unknown to him, and the references to ships and the dangers of the sea are frequent enough to suggest some personal experience of them. We may therefore accept the view that he took part in trade in his youth, and it is probable that he gained a reputation for sagacity and faithfulness. He was engaged by Khadījah, a widow of some means, to conduct business on her behalf in the Syrian caravan, and on his return she let it be known to him that she would regard him favourably as a suitor. The marriage which took place when he was about twenty-five proved a happy one, and relieved him to some extent from poverty. He seems never to have been, at any rate during his Meccan residence, really wealthy; cf. XXV, 8 f.

When he was about forty years of age, that is, *c.* A.D. 610, he began a religious mission in his native town of Meccah. The well-known story of his Call to be a prophet cannot, unfortunately, be accepted as historical. It is weakly attested, and contains anachronisms and alien elements.[1] For the beginnings of Muhammad's mission we are largely dependent for information on what we can infer from the Qur'ān itself.

The period of his religious activity in Meccah extended to ten or twelve years, but there are few definite events mentioned as having happened during that time; in any case, as his rôle was that of a preacher and teacher of a new

[1] See pp. 18 and 31.

religion, his deliverances were hortatory and didactic, and had little reference to contemporary events. Again we are for the most part dependent upon the Qur'ān itself for light upon the development of his mission, and there is room for a good deal of difference of opinion. The view here taken, for which it is hoped the reasons will appear later, may be briefly summarised as follows. Muhammad claimed to be the Messenger of God to his own people and town. He began by advocating monotheism, the worship of one God upon whose power and bounty man was dependent, and in gratitude to whom he owed obedience and the generous use of the good things provided for him. The appearance of such a messenger was nothing new. Each community had had its messenger, and the rejection of the messenger had meant the destruction of the community which had refused to believe. Alongside this, not displacing it, appears later the doctrine of a Day of Judgment, at which men will be judged as individuals, and receive the reward of their conduct by being consigned either to heaven or to hell, which are described with much detail. Borrowing from Jewish and Christian sources is at this stage very evident, and the attitude to previous monotheists is friendly. The chief religious rite instituted in Meccah was the *ṣalāt*, or ritual prayer. Morning and evening are the times spoken of, and night prayers are recommended. Almsgiving and provision for the poor, the widow, and the orphan are advocated as recognition of God's bounty.

Muhammad's preaching in Meccah produced comparatively little effect. A small number believed, mostly of the poorer classes. Attacks upon the Meccan gods at length drew down persecution upon his followers. A number of them emigrated to Abyssinia. He himself and his supporters who belonged to Meccan families were protected by the danger of starting blood-feuds, but the situation was uncomfortable. An abortive attempt at a compromise with polytheism, which is alleged by Tradition, seems to have left a trace in surah LIII. Muhammad now lost hope of Meccah and began to look around for another settlement. He tried Ṭā'if without success. Negotiations with parties from Yathrib (Medinah) led, however, to agreement. In September A.D. 622 (the first certain date of his career) he left Meccah and settled in Medinah, whither most of his supporters had already gone. This is known as the Hijrah (Hegira).

In Medinah, Muhammad occupied a public position. He and his supporters had been brought in as a balance between the rivalries of the clans of Aus and Khazraj. He thus found scope for his remarkable political gifts. Of more immediate importance from the point of view of the Qur'ān was his relationship to the Jews, of whom there were strong colonies in the neighbourhood of Medinah. He expected their support as monotheists, and showed himself willing to learn and adapt his religious practice to theirs. In spite of this, however, they rejected his prophetic claims, and ridiculed him. They opposed his political designs. His friendly attitude changed to hostility. His revulsion from the religion of the People of the Book to a purified Arab religion was marked by the change of *qiblah* (direction of prayer) from Jerusalem to Meccah, somewhere about the middle of the year II of the Hijrah (December 623).

Hostilities had meanwhile been developing with the Meccans. " Those who had disbelieved " deserved destruction. Besides, the needs of the Muhājirīn (the emigrants who had left Meccah and come to Medinah) were pressing. Small expeditions began to molest the Meccan caravans. Many of his followers disliked this new warlike attitude, and the people of Medinah were naturally doubtful where it would lead. Further difficulty was caused by an attack on a small caravan at Nakhlah at the beginning of Rajab II, which raised the question of fighting in the sacred months. An ambitious attempt to intercept one of the chief Meccan caravans returning from Syria led to a battle at the wells of Badr, in which Muhammad's following of a little over 300 men defeated a Quraish army of nearly 1000, Ramaḍān II, February 624. This greatly enhanced the Prophet's prestige and confirmed his claims. But the booty had not been so great as had been expected, and difficulties arose as to the division of it. The expulsion of one of the Jewish colonies, the Banī Qainuqā', from Medinah followed in a little over a month's time.

The Quraish were known to be preparing to avenge their defeat; Muhammad was building up his strength, regulating his community, and making appeals for unity and for contributions. In Shawwāl III, March 625, a large Meccan force appeared before Medinah. The feeling in the town was in favour of remaining on the defensive. Muhammad ultimately decided to accept the Quraish challenge. He marched out and took up his position at Uḥud, a hill to the north of the town; on the way, however, a portion of his army broke off and returned to the town. The Moslems were defeated, but the Quraish, having no quarrel with Medinah, withdrew. Muhammad, recovering from a slight wound and rallying some of his forces, followed, and claimed a victory. His position was, nevertheless, badly shaken, and for some months he was occupied in restoring morale in Medinah. The expulsion of the Banī Naḍīr, another Jewish colony, in the month of II Rabī' of the year IV, September 625, may be taken as a sign that his ascendancy had been re-established. Moslem propaganda and raiding were resumed. The Meccans, finding their trade still being interfered with, formed a great coalition against Medinah, which, towards the end of the year V, brought together a large force outside the town. Muhammad had prepared a trench for the defence of the town. This novelty in Arab warfare nonplussed the attackers. As they lay inactive, the unity of the coalition began to wear out, and a storm of wind and rain finally dispersed it. The last remaining Jewish colony in Medinah had been lured into expressing sympathy with the attackers, and was immediately attacked and compelled to surrender. The men were ruthlessly slaughtered, Dhū l-Ḥijjah V, March 627.

A year later Muhammad thought himself strong enough to force his way into Meccah. His Bedouin allies, however, failed him. Professing peaceable intentions he set out, ostensibly to perform the pilgrimage. He found his way blocked by Meccan forces, and halting at the borders of the *ḥaram*, at Ḥudaibiyah, he entered into negotiations. The treaty here made was a disappointment to his followers, but really marked the end of Meccan supremacy. It was followed in the beginning of the next year by an attack on the Jewish colony of Khaibar, Muḥarram VII, May 628. The peaceful pilgrimage provided for in the treaty of Ḥudaibiyah took place in the pilgrimage month of that year, April 629. In an expedition to extend his influence northward he unexpectedly met strong Byzantine resistance and was defeated at Mu'tah, I Jumādā VIII, September 629. Meccan influence had been waning, and some leading Meccans had already joined Muhammad in Medinah. A great expedition was now got together to overwhelm the town. Negotiations meanwhile took place, and Meccah was entered almost without fighting, Ramaḍān VIII, December 629. The Ka'bah was cleansed from idols, but the townspeople, most of whom accepted Islam, were kindly dealt with.

Almost immediately, Muhammad was menaced by a combination of Arab tribes, among whom his march south had aroused suspicions. The Moslems met them at Ḥunain, and at the first onset were almost swept from the field. The veteran Medinan troops, however, held firm, and the others rallied round them. The Arabs were defeated and fled in confusion leaving a great amount of booty in Moslem hands, Shawwāl VIII, January 630. The prestige of the Prophet was now established throughout Arabia, and deputations began to come in from tribes far and near. The conditions for their adherence were, the acceptance of Islam, the destruction of idols, and the payment of the *zakāt* or tax for the support of the Moslem community.

An expedition towards the Syrian border, known as the expedition to Tabūk, probably designed to avenge the defeat at Mu'tah, led to nothing of importance, Rajab IX, October 630. This was the last warlike expedition in which the Prophet took part. He led the pilgrimage of the year X, March 632. Another expedition, destined for the North, was being prepared, when he took ill and after a few days died, I Rabī' XI, June 632.

Note on Chronology.—The Arab year was a lunar one, but was kept roughly in accord with the seasons by the insertion of an extra month (*an-nasy*), every three years or so. Muhammad abolished this practice, IX, 36 f.; thus making the year purely lunar. When, in the caliphate of ʿOmar, the Moslem era was established, the beginning of the year in which the Hijrah (Migration to Medinah) took place was taken as the beginning of year I. This corresponds to 16th July A.D. 622. Approximately 33 Moslem years are equal to 32 Christian years. The names and order of the Arabic months are:

1. Muḥarram (Holy month).
2. Ṣafar.
3. ar-Rabīʿ al-awwal (I Rabīʿ).
4. ar-Rabīʿ ath-thāni (II Rabīʿ).
5. Jumādā al-ʾūlā (I Jumādā).
6. Jumādā al-ākhirah (II Jumādā).
7. Rajab (Holy month).
8. Shaʿbān.
9. Ramaḍān.
10. Shawwāl.
11. Dhū l-Qaʿdah (Holy month).
12. Dhū l-Ḥijjah (Holy month).

MUHAMMAD'S CHARACTER AND AIMS

As will have appeared from the above sketch, Muhammad's activity as a religious teacher and reformer fell into two sections of approximately equal length, that in Meccah and that in Medinah. His situation was very different in the two periods. In Meccah he had no recognised position, and, while he gained some adherents, they were neither numerous, nor, except one or two individuals, influential, and their position became gradually more and more untenable. In Medinah he had from the first a position of influence as holding the balance between two hostile factions. That position may not have been exactly official, and was at first precarious, but the ever-present fear of recurring strife disposed the leaders of the factions to accept his advice, and prevented those who were doubtful of his policies, " those in whose hearts was disease ", taking resolute measures against him. Thus, in spite of the set-back occasioned by the defeat at Uḥud, his influence grew, and by the end of his life had extended far across Arabia. This difference in the Prophet's position is naturally reflected in the style, tone and subject of the Qur'ān. But the line between Meccan and Medinan style must not be too rigidly drawn. The statesman of

Medinah was not necessarily incapable of producing passages in the style of the religious propagandist of Meccah.

On the other hand, there was more development in Muhammad's ideas and opinions than has usually been allowed for. It has indeed been generally recognised that he began as a messenger to his native town of Meccah, and that his conception of the scope of his mission extended to include the Arabs, if not mankind as a whole. But it was not only in this respect that his ideas changed and expanded. His knowledge of Judaism and Christianity and of the contents of their Scriptures was meagre to begin with, but was diligently increased, not by way of study and reading—for though not illiterate he was certainly no bookman—but by oral enquiry as opportunity brought him into contact with people who could give, or professed to be able to give, information. Muhammad's teaching retained throughout its fundamental character, but there is hardly an aspect of it which was not altered and enriched by this increasing acquaintance with earlier religious ideas as time went on. That has been dealt with in my *Origin of Islam in its Christian Environment* ; the following treatment of the Qur'ān will bring it out more clearly.

We shall also see more clearly than before to what extent Muhammad, prompted, as he would have said, by Allah, was himself the architect of the success of Islam. Critical analysis of the Qur'ān brings out its effectiveness for the purpose of religious awakening, for which it was originally designed. And the more we are able to place the political deliverances which it contains in their historical setting, the better we realise the insight and ability of the man who delivered them. Inflexible of purpose, yet ready to temporise and make concessions, diplomatic almost to the verge of dishonesty, he steered his sometimes devious way to the establishment of the worship of the One God in Medinah and all Arabia. One feels that, without him, the struggle would, more than once, have been lost, if indeed it had ever been begun.

There were, of course, various circumstances which contributed to his success and prepared the way for Islam. The wealth and civilisation of the Christian lands which surrounded Arabia exercised a glamour upon the Arab mind that made it not inhospitable to a religion similar to that which prevailed there. The hold of the ancient paganism on the Arabs had been loosened. In Meccah, which profited by its religious position, there was no doubt an interest in preserving the customary rites. But in Medinah paganism seems to have crumbled easily; the presence of influential colonies of Jews had no doubt helped to predispose the people to the acceptance of monotheism. When, with the change of *qiblah*, and the adoption of the Kaʿbah as the centre of Islam, the enlightened religion of the People of the Book had been combined with ancient Arab practice, the demands of Arab patriotism were satisfied. There must have been many minds in Arabia to whom the idea of an inclusive brotherhood overriding the tribal divisions which gave rise to so much strife and bloodshed, was attractive. But tradition and custom, tribal pride and ambition, died hard; and but for the man who had conceived the idea, and guided the infant community, Islam would undoubtedly have been crushed. In some respects it was perhaps a pity that the success of Islam was based upon temporal power and recourse to war. On the other hand, but for his adroit use of the influence which came to him and the military force which he built upon it, the Arabs would not have been united under the banner of Islam, and the history of the world would, at least, have been very different.

It has sometimes been held that a man so gifted for politics must have had this political aim before him from the start. But this is to confound the secondary result with the primary impulse. Muhammad was perhaps more akin to the ecclesiastic than to the pious devotee, more the organiser of a religion than the original seeker after truth, but there is no doubt that the impulse which set him upon his mission was a religious one, and that the religious aim was with him the overruling motive all through. He sought and wielded power, but it was for the furthering of monotheism and Islam. The question of what induced Muhammad to take up his mission and proclaim himself as the Messenger of God to the Arabs is so intimately bound up with the problem of the chronological arrangement of the Qur'ān that it can hardly be treated apart from that. But it may be pointed out here that in no chronological arrangement which has been suggested does the political motive appear early. Further, wherever the Qur'ān speaks of previous messengers, they are represented as having come with a religious message, a call to the worship of One God; and it is agreed that the accounts of these predecessors are largely moulded by Muhammad's own experience. It is therefore as a religious personality that he is to be regarded. In fact it may be said that without a deep realisation of the religious fear which drove him forward and the religious conviction which gave him strength, it is impossible to understand the personality of Muhammad.

MUHAMMAD'S INSPIRATION

One point calls for fuller treatment here, because it has affected men's judgment upon the character of Muhammad, and has, besides, intimate bearings upon the whole conception and composition of the Qur'ān. Muhammad claimed to be a prophet, and to speak in the name of God. It will perhaps appear in what follows that he was much more modest in his claims, at any rate to begin with, than either Moslem or Western scholars have assumed. It was, in fact, only as he measured himself against the ideas of Jews and Christians as to the authority and inspiration of prophets that his claims grew. Probably it was not until after he had transferred to Medinah that he claimed the full authority of a prophet. Still, he did claim that position and authority, and long before that time he had claimed to speak in the name of God, and had even put forth deliverances purporting to be in the actual words of God. How are we to understand this? Did he make false claims? Or was there some reality behind the assertion? What was the nature of his inspiration?

The answer formerly so frequently given that he was a false prophet who pretended to receive messages from God, we may discard, if for no other reason than that it is too simple. There is sufficient evidence in the Qur'ān itself, apart from Tradition, that the claim brought upon him ridicule and even persecution, against which only some real belief could have held its ground. He may have been mistaken in the interpretation of his experience, but there must have been something which led him to the belief that he received messages from a divine source. We must try to gather what information we can as to how he thought these messages were given to him.

Since Carlyle laughed out of court the idea of an impostor being the founder of one of the world's great religions, various attempts have been made to save Muhammad's sincerity—sometimes at the expense of his sanity. Weil seeks to prove that he suffered from epilepsy. Sprenger, not content with this, dilates on the phenomena of hysteria, from which, he suggests, Muhammad suffered in addition Muir retains something of the false-prophet idea, and pictures the earnest high-souled messenger and preacher succumbing to the wiles of Satan for the sake of success. Margoliouth has no qualms about accusing him of having deliberately mystified the people, pointing to the phenomena of spiritualism as showing how easily human beings fall into that dishonesty. Noeldeke, while insisting on the reality of Muhammad's prophetic inspiration, and rejecting the idea that he suffered from epilepsy, thinks that he was subject to overpowering fits of emotion which led him to believe that he was under divine influences. In all this perhaps more attention has been paid to the statements of Tradition than to the evidence of the Qur'ān itself; and surely too little has been allowed for the fact that the Muhammad whom we know best was to all appearance healthy both in body and in mind. It seems incredible that a person subject to epilepsy, or hysteria, or even ungovernable fits of emotion, could have been the active leader of expeditions, or the cool far-seeing guide of a city-state and growing religious community, which we know Muhammad to have been. Here again we have to depend mainly on the Qur'ān itself, and accept Tradition only in so far as it is in harmony with the results of Qur'ān study.

Now the Qur'ān gives no support to the existence of any

diseased condition in the Prophet. It chronicles, apparently without reserve, the gibes and reproaches of his opponents, but there is no mention of anything of that kind. They do indeed say that he is *majnūn*, but that simply means that they thought his conduct crazy, or that his utterances were inspired by a jinn, as those of the soothsayers were supposed to be. Sometimes one almost feels that Muhammad himself was not quite sure on that point. But that his opponents could point to any evident signs of disease is very improbable; had that been so, we should most likely have heard of it.

One of the latest and clearest accounts of the matter in the Qur'ān is in II, 91, where Gabriel is said to have brought it (the revelation) down upon the Prophet's heart, with the permission of Allah. That this was the explanation which Muhammad gave out and allowed to be understood in his Medinan days is certain. Tradition is unanimous on the point that it was Gabriel who was the agent of revelation. But when Tradition carries this back to the very beginning, and associates Gabriel with the Call, we are struck by the fact that Gabriel is only twice mentioned in the Qur'ān, both times in Medinan passages. Gabriel, we suspect, is a later interpretation of something which Muhammad had at first understood otherwise. It is to be noted that the verse above referred to makes no claim that Gabriel appeared in visible form. Muhammad claims to have seen a vision on two occasions, see LIII, 1-12, 13-18. Strictly read, these passages imply visions of Allah; but in LXXXI, 15-29, the vision is re-interpreted as that of an angel—an indication that Muhammad himself interpreted some things in his experience differently at different times. Having at first assumed that he had seen Allah in person, he has now realised the impossibility of that and concluded that it must have been a messenger from Allah, that is, an angel. Similarly with the reception of his messages, he may have interpreted the matter differently at the beginning from the interpretation he put upon it in Medinah. That the visions, however we may explain them, were to Muhammad real enough, there is no reason to doubt. But they stand by themselves; he makes no claim to have seen other visions. There is just as little in the Qur'ān to support the supposition, which Tor Andrae adopts, that he heard voices. In XLII, 50 ff. both the visible appearance of Allah and the hearing of His voice are rejected, and the explanation adopted is that He may speak by ' suggestion ' or send a messenger to ' suggest '.

What then is meant by ' suggest ' and ' suggestion '? The verb *awḥā* and the noun *waḥy* have become the technical terms in Moslem theology for the communication of the revelation to Muhammad, and have come to imply the recitation of the words of the Qur'ān to him by the angel Gabriel. In the Qur'ān itself they are indeed the words commonly used in that connection, but they are not confined to it. The word *awḥā* is used in XIX, 12 of Zachariah, who having become dumb signed (*awḥā*) to the people that they should glorify God. Satans of jinn and men ' suggest ' things to each other, VI, 121. The recipient of *waḥy*, even from Allah, is not always a prophet, or even a human being. Allah ' suggests ' to the bee to take houses for herself in the hills and trees and the arbours which men erect, XVI, 70. The earth gives up its dead because its Lord has ' suggested ' to it so to do, XCIX, 2. Allah ' suggested ' to each of the seven heavens its special function, XLI, 11. Even when the recipient is a prophet, what is communicated is usually not the words of a revelation, but a practical line of conduct, something to do, not to say. Thus it is ' suggested ' to Noah to build the ark, and he is to build it under Allah's eyes and at His ' suggestion ', XI, 39, XVII, 41. To Moses it is ' suggested ' to set out with his people by night, XX, 79, XXVI, 52, to strike the sea with his staff, XXVI, 63, to strike the rock with his staff, VII, 160. To Muhammad himself it is ' suggested ' that he should follow the religion of Abraham, XVI, 124. These practical ' suggestions ' are often, it is true, formulated in direct speech, as if a form of words had been put into a person's mind. There are cases too in which the formula has reference to doctrine rather than to conduct; for example, " Your God is One God ", XVIII, 110, XXI, 108, XLI, 5. But the formula is usually quite short, the sort of phrase, it may be remarked, which might flash into a person's mind after consideration of a matter as the final summing up and solution of it. There are indeed a few passages in which the verb seems to mean the communication of somewhat lengthy pieces to the prophet; for example, III, 39, XI, 51, XII, 103. But even in them the actual verbal communication of the stories is not quite certainly implied. The fundamental sense of the word as used in the Qur'ān seems to be the communication of an idea by some quick suggestion or prompting, by, as we might say, a flash of inspiration. This agrees with what is given in the dictionaries (see *Lisān al-'Arab*, s.v.) which implies that haste or quickness is part of the connotation of the root.

The frequent use of this term in connection with the Prophet's inspiration makes us suspect that there was something short and sudden about it. If now we suppose that Muhammad was one of those brooding spirits to whom, after a longer or shorter period of intense absorption in a problem, the solution comes in a flash, as if by suggestion from without, his use of the word would be intelligible. Nor is this merely a supposition. All the evidence goes to show that the Prophet, accessible enough in the ordinary intercourse of men, had yet something withdrawn and separate about him. In the ultimate issue he took counsel with himself and followed his own decisions. If decisions did come to him in this way, it was perhaps natural that he should attribute them to outside suggestion. The experience was mysterious to him. He had before him the example of the *kāhins*, who probably claimed that they spoke by outside prompting. Once or twice, probably near the beginning of his mission, when his hesitations had caused him more than usually intense and long-continued mental exertion, the decision had come to him accompanied by a vision. He had assumed that it was Allah who had appeared to him and suggested that he should speak to the people in public. It is to be noted that in LIII, where these visions are described, nothing is said about the Qur'ān. It is simply a 'suggestion' which came to him, and it is his 'speaking' which he is explaining and defending. It was to that, then, that the 'suggestion' referred.

But if he was to speak to the people, he had to find words

in which to speak. That he took trouble about this we know from LXXIII, 1-8, where we see the Prophet at the work of composing the Qur'ān, choosing the night-hours as being " strongest in impression and most just in speech ", that is, the time when ideas are clearest, and fitting words most readily found.[1] A similar experience of the words coming in the end after effort and meditation, easily as if by inspiration, may well have led him to extend the idea of suggestion from without to the actual words of his deliverances. A curious little passage, which has been preserved as a scrap in LXXV, 16 ff., seems to show him deliberately cultivating this : " Move not thy tongue that thou mayest do it quickly ; Ours it is to collect it and recite it ; when we recite it follow thou the recitation ; then Ours it is to explain it ". This has always been taken as referring to the reception of the Qur'ān, and if we try to get behind the usual mechanical interpretation we can picture Muhammad in the throes of composition. He has been seeking words which will flow and rhyme and express his meaning, repeating phrases audibly to himself, trying to force the continuation before the whole has become clear. He is being admonished or, as we should say, he realises and admonishes himself, that this is not the way ; he must not " press ", but wait for the inspiration which will give the words without this impatient effort to find them. When his mind has calmed, and the whole has taken shape, the words will come ; and when they do come, he must take them as they are given him. If they are somewhat cryptic—as they may well happen to be—they can be explained later. If that be the proper interpretation of the passage, it throws light on a characteristic of the Qur'ān which has often been remarked on, namely, its disjointedness. For passages composed in such fashion must almost of necessity be comparatively short.

This, then, it seems to me, is the thread of reality that runs through Muhammad's claim to inspiration. It has analogies to the experience which poets refer to as the coming of the muse, or more closely to what religious people describe as the coming of guidance after meditation and waiting upon

[1] Bell, *Origin of Islam in its Christian Environment*, p. 97 f.

God. " Guidance " is in fact one of his favourite words for the message, though it is used in rather a different sense. This experience he interpreted in various ways. At first he assumed that it was Allah who spoke to him, just as he had assumed that it was Allah who had appeared to him in his visions. Then, according to XLII, 50 ff., this idea was rejected in favour of the idea of a spirit implanted within him. Later, when through increasing familiarity with Jewish and Christian ideas he had learned of angels as the messengers of God, he assumed that it was angels who brought the message. Finally, he adopted Gabriel as the special angel who prompted him on Allah's behalf. We shall find passages of the Qur'ān illustrating all these various ideas. But always the essence of the experience is the same : he was prompted, ' suggestions ' were made to him, the message was brought down upon his heart. That these promptings came ultimately from a divine source, however mediated, he was convinced. He may, indeed, have had occasional doubts. He realised, perhaps as a result of the false step which he made in recognising the pagan deities as intercessors, and of other mistakes which he may have made, that Satan might take a hand in the prompting, XXII, 51. The assurances that he was not mad, or prompted by a jinn, may have been partly meant for himself. But on the whole he held firmly to his belief, and upon it he built up his claims to authority. These were in some respects modest enough. He was only a human being to whom ' suggestions ' were made, XVIII, 110, XLI, 5. But this guidance by ' suggestion ' was all that the prophets had experienced ; only to Moses had God spoken directly, XVII, 103. Thus to all the authority of a prophet he could lay claim.

That this experience of ' suggestion ' or ' guidance ' is a real one, no one who has ever become deeply absorbed in a difficult problem will deny. But the habit of expecting such experiences, and the attempt to induce them, are not without their dangers. We cannot force the answer which we wish, or indeed any answer, at the time we wish it. Muhammad seems to have experienced this also, XVIII, 23. It is when the mind is more or less passive that such 'suggestions' come, but it makes a great difference whether this passive attitude is the result of a heavy strain upon the mental and spiritual powers, or is cultivated as a state of more or less mental vacancy. Between these two poles there is the danger of meditation becoming brooding over passing troubles, or of allowing too easy a response to external stimuli. Of some of these dangers Muhammad seems to have, at times, been conscious, as is shown by V, 101, XXII, 51. But it may be questioned whether he always guarded sufficiently against them. Once he had become accustomed to the idea of being guided in this way, he cultivated the attitude of receiving such messages, and often mistook his own brooding reaction to events for the divine afflatus. In later life when events pressed upon him and decisions were imperative, and questions arose which he could not avoid answering, he did no doubt try to force the revelation, and acquired facility in getting the answer which he desired. Nor need we deny that he was capable of practising a certain amount of mystification regarding his communications from Allah. He surrounded them with some degree of awe and mystery. This does not detract from the sincerity of his own belief in them. They were mysterious to himself, and if they were what he believed them to be, they were worthy of awe. He regarded them always as something separate and distinct. Nor were they always, even in his later days, in accord with his own natural desires. As, at the first, he maintained that he did not speak of his own desire, so, in Medinah, we find him being exhorted to steadfastness when his inclination was to compromise, urged to policies which he felt to be difficult, and taken to task for things which he had done or omitted to do. That could not have been altogether a pose.

Of the essential sincerity of Muhammad there need be no question. We need not, however, go to the other extreme and picture him as a modern saint. The age was a rude one to our ideas, even in the most enlightened parts of the world, and Arabia was not one of these.

CHAPTER II

THE ORIGIN OF THE QUR'ĀN

ITS DELIVERY, COLLECTION AND AUTHENTICITY

Theological Doctrine.—According to the received doctrine of Islam the Qur'ān is eternal; it is the uncreated Word of God. The doctrine is thus stated by Abū Ḥanīfah: "The Qur'ān is the speech of Allah, written in the copies, preserved in the memories, recited by the tongues, revealed to the Prophet. Our pronouncing, writing and reciting the Qur'ān is created, whereas the Qur'ān itself is uncreated" (*Al-fiqh al-akbar*, as translated by Wensinck, *The Muslim Creed*, p. 189). That is how the Logos-idea, which in Christianity is the basis of the doctrine of the eternally begotten Son, takes shape in Islam. The Qur'ān is the Eternal Word in book-form. More popularly and concretely, if with less theological exactitude, the original of the Qur'ān is thought of as a book preserved in (the seventh) heaven in the presence of God. This is assumed to be what is meant by the preserved tablet, *lawḥ maḥfūẓ*, spoken of in LXXXV, 22. Sometimes it is thought of as having been sent down to the nearest heaven on the night of power, *lailat al-qadar*, described in XCVII, so as to be available for revelation to the Prophet by the angel Gabriel. Muhammad is thus not the author, but only the recipient of the Qur'ān.

The Delivery of the Qur'ān.—This high doctrine of the divine origin of the Qur'ān does not, however, extend to its present order and arrangement. Popularly, of course, that is taken as fixed and settled for all time. But Moslem scholars have always recognised that the present arrangement is not the order in which the passages of which it is composed were revealed. The Qur'ān was not revealed all at once, but in separate pieces, XXV, 34. Tradition distributes these pieces over some twenty years. Apart from a break, *fatrah*, of two years immediately after his Call, the revelations are represented as coming upon Muhammad at frequent intervals up to the time of his death. Practically all passages that can be interpreted as referring to contemporary events or circumstances have special 'occasions' assigned to them. These 'occasions' are not always agreed upon, and to a critical eye are often founded rather upon imaginative exegesis than upon recollections handed down. But Tradition does thus recognise the close relation between the Qur'ān and the personal history of the Prophet. That he recited the revelations is attested by the Qur'ān as well as by Tradition. The prevailing view is that the words of the revelations were given him by the angel Gabriel, and he, having memorised them, or having had them impressed upon his memory, recited them to the people. With regard to the preservation of these revelations, all the traditions agree that Muhammad did not write them himself; several speak of his having employed others to write them, and certain persons are named as having done so (N-S., I, p. 46). This seems to imply that, at any rate in the later years of his life, he kept a written record of the revelations, as indeed the nature of the passages almost necessitates his having done. But when we come to the traditions dealing with the collection of the Qur'ān, the impression we get as to the condition in which it had been left at the Prophet's death is quite different.

The Collection of the Qur'ān.—The tradition as to the collection of the Qur'ān after Muhammad's death seems to assume that up to that time there had been no authoritative record of the revelations. Some passages had been used in the ritual prayer, and would of course be well known. For the rest, some believers had memorised them, some more, some less; and some had written out portions for their own use. The tradition says that in the battle of Yamāmah, a year or so after the Prophet's death, so many 'readers' of the Qur'ān, that is, persons who had it, or portions of it, by heart, were killed, that 'Omar b. al-Khaṭṭāb (afterwards the second caliph) became alarmed lest some of the Qur'ān should be lost altogether unless something were done to preserve it. He therefore suggested to Abū Bakr, the caliph, that the Qur'ān should be collected and written down. Abū Bakr at first refused to do what the Prophet himself had not done, but was finally persuaded. He commissioned Zaid b. Thābit, who had already acted as one of the Prophet's secretaries, to do what 'Omar had suggested. Zaid then collected the Qur'ān " from pieces of paper, stones, palm-leaves, shoulder-blades, ribs, bits of leather, and from the hearts of men ", that is, from their memories and the various kinds of writing material which had been used for writing portions of it down. He copied out what he collected on sheets (*ṣuḥuf*), and when his work was finished he handed it over to the caliph.

Criticism of this Tradition.—Apart from the fact that there are, as we have seen, traditions which imply that the Prophet kept some record of his revelations, this tradition is open to certain criticisms. There are many discrepancies in the various versions of the tradition. They are not even unanimous as to the originator of the idea: generally it is 'Omar who is said to have been the moving spirit in the matter, but sometimes it is said to have been Abū Bakr who ordered it on his own initiative. Discrepancies are, however, a common feature of often-repeated traditions, and we cannot attach great weight to them. But the reason given for the step, namely the death of a large number of 'readers' in the battle of Yamāmah, has also been questioned. For in the lists of those who fell in that campaign, very few (according to Schwally,[1] only two) are mentioned who were likely to have had much of the Qur'ān by heart. Those killed were mostly recent converts. Besides, according to the tradition itself, a good deal of the Qur'ān was already written in some form or other, so that the death of some of those who could recite it from memory need not have given rise to the fear that much of the Qur'ān would be lost. Thirdly, an official collection of this kind might have been expected to have had wider authority attributed to it than we anywhere find evidence of. Other collections of the Qur'ān seem to have

[1] N-S., II, p. 20.

been regarded as authoritative in different provinces. The disputes which led to the recension of the Qur'ān under 'Othman could hardly have arisen if there had been an official codex in the caliph's possession to which reference could have been made. And the way in which 'Omar himself is represented in other traditions as insisting that the "verse of stoning"[1] was in the Qur'ān, is hardly consistent with his having in his possession an official collection. Lastly, and most significant of all, the *ṣuḥuf* on which Zaid wrote the Qur'ān were, at the time when the revision came to be made, in the keeping of Ḥafṣah. Now Ḥafṣah was 'Omar's daughter, and we are apparently to assume that 'Omar, having become caliph by the time Zaid finished his work, the *ṣuḥuf* were handed to him, and from him passed to his daughter. But if Zaid's collection were an official one, it seems hardly probable that it would pass out of official keeping, even into the hands of the caliph's daughter. That Ḥafṣah had a copy of the Qur'ān on *ṣuḥuf* seems certain; but it hardly appears that it was an official copy made in the official way that Tradition asserts.

Pre-'Othmanic Qur'āns.—It is of course possible that Zaid b. Thābit did make a collection of the Qur'ān. Schwally[2] suggests that he did so on Ḥafṣah's commission, but gives no very cogent reason why Ḥafṣah in particular should have desired to have a copy of the Qur'ān made. Quite a number of people are said to have collected the Qur'ān in these early days. Of these early collections little is known, though variant readings are sometimes quoted as having occurred in them. There are, however, four collections, or editions, of the Qur'ān which, in the interval between Muhammad's death and the formation of a definitive text, seem to have been current in different districts and to have been regarded as authoritative there. They are (1) that of Ubayy b. Ka'b, whose readings are said to have been followed by the people of Syria; (2) that of 'Abdallah b. Mas'ūd, the great authority on Islam in Kūfah, whose readings were accepted by the people of that district; (3) that of Abū Mūsā al-Ash'arī, who was associated mainly with Baṣrah; and (4) that of

[1] See below, p. 48. [2] N-S., II, p. 22.

Miqdad b. ʿAmr, whose readings are said to have been accepted by the people of Ḥimṣ.

No copies of these collections, or editions, have survived. Concerning those of Abū Mūsā and Miqdad b. ʿAmr we know very little. Of the other two, some information is given by later writers. In addition to a considerable number of variant readings attributed to them, which indeed affect mainly the vowels and punctuation but in some cases affect the consonantal text, we have lists of the surahs (chapters) in each. The order of the surahs is different in each from that of the official Qur'ān, and from that of the other. But on the whole, as in the official Qur'ān, the long surahs come first. The names of the surahs, in the main, agree, and, while that might have been due to the later transcribers of the lists having used the names by which the surahs were ordinarily known, there is no indication that the actual surahs differed from those usually accepted. Ibn Masʿūd did not include the two last surahs—they are of the nature of prayers or charms, and may never have been intended to form part of the actual Qur'ān. The first surah, the *Fātiḥah*, is also a prayer, placed at the beginning of the book. Whether Ibn Masʿūd included it in his Qur'ān or not, is not quite certain. Ubayy seems to have included all three, the first and the two last, and to have had in addition two others which are not in our present Qur'ān. The text of these is given by later writers They are short prayers and, to judge by their language, are not Qur'ānic.[1]

On the whole, then, the information we have regarding these independent Qur'āns (if independent they were) does not lead us to suspect that there was any great variation in the actual contents of the Qur'ān in the period immediately after the Prophet's death. The order of the surahs was perhaps not fixed, and the reading varied somewhat; of other differences we have no evidence. The position is obscure, but, as far as we can make out, the Qur'ān at this period consisted pretty much of what was afterwards included in the official recension. It seems reasonable to suppose that such copies as existed were somehow related to what lay

[1] Cf. N-S., II, p. 34 ff.

behind that recension. As to how or why these collections were made, Tradition gives us no information. But as the teaching of the Qur'ān was one of the duties of the agents of Islam even in the Prophet's life-time, we may suspect that these agents were not left to depend entirely on their memories, but that some written record of the revelations was made and furnished to them.

The 'Othmanic Recension.—The tradition as to what led up to the next step in the fixing of the form of the Qur'ān implies that serious differences of reading did exist, in the copies of the Qur'ān current in the various districts. During the expedition against Armenia and Azerbaijān, we are told, disputes concerning the reading of the Qur'ān arose amongst the troops, who were drawn partly from Syria and partly from Iraq. The disputes were serious enough to lead the general, Ḥudhaifah, to lay the matter before the caliph, 'Othman, and to urge him to take steps to put an end to these differences. The caliph took counsel with the leaders of Islam, and finally commissioned Zaid b. Thābit to revise the Qur'ān. With Zaid were associated three members of noble Meccan families. One of the principles to be followed, according to the Tradition, was that, in case of difficulty as to the reading, the dialect of Quraish, the tribe to which the Prophet belonged, was to be given the preference. The whole Qur'ān was carefully revised and compared with the *ṣuḥuf*, which had been in Ḥafṣah's keeping and were returned to her when the work was finished. Thus an authoritative text of the Qur'ān was established. A number of copies were made and distributed to the main centres of Islam. As to the exact number of these standard codices, and the places to which they were sent, Tradition varies; but probably one copy was retained in Medinah, and one was sent to each of the towns, Kūfah, Baṣrah and Damascus, and possibly also to Meccah. Previously existing copies are said to have been then destroyed, so that the text of all subsequent copies of the Qur'ān should be based upon those standard codices.

This revision under 'Othman, which may be dated somewhere between the year XXX and 'Othman's death in

XXXV, or about twenty years after Muhammad's death, is the cardinal point in the formation of what we may call the canon of the Qur'ān. Whatever may have been the form of the Qur'ān before that time, and as to that Tradition is by no means clear, we can be fairly certain that the book retains still the form then established. That recension fixed the number and order of the surahs or chapters, and it established the consonantal text. Arabic had as yet no means of indicating the vowels, beyond the use of weak consonants in the text for the indication of long vowels. It is also questionable to what extent the diacritical points which distinguish different consonants of the Arabic alphabet were then in use. There remained therefore considerable room for variations in reading. As a matter of fact, we find in the history of the text of the Qur'ān a great number of variant readings. But the great bulk of these affect only the vocalisation and the pointing of the letters ; comparatively few affect the outline of the consonantal text. We hear of a later revision of the Qur'ān in the reign of 'Abd-al-malik, associated with the name of Al-Ḥajjāj, the famous governor of Iraq. It was no doubt an attempt to fix the vocalisation and to obtain a uniform reading. There were even later attempts to do that; but they were never completely successful. It became orthodox doctrine that seven varying ways of reading the Qur'ān were canonical; and, though the tendency towards uniformity still operates, that remains the orthodox view. There can, however, be no doubt that all these seven ways of reading the Qur'ān are based upon the 'Othmanic revision.

Authenticity of the Qur'ān.—If now we ask what guarantee there is that this revision reproduced the actual revelations delivered by Muhammad, the answer will depend largely on actual study of the Qur'an itself, and on the extent to which what is contained in it approves itself to historical criticism as fitting into the Prophet's life. But we may stress the fact that this revision was based on written documents previously existing. The official collection by express authority of the caliph Abū Bakr is, as we have seen, somewhat doubtful. But a mass of written documents of some kind was in Ḥafṣah's possession. Of that fact there is no doubt. If we reject the assumption that they were an official collection made by Zaid, we must find some other explanation of what they were. It is clear that they were regarded as authoritative, and were taken as the basis of 'Othman's Qur'ān. Other collections of the Qur'ān were in existence, and there must have been a considerable number of people who knew them, or parts of them, by heart. It is not likely that any great changes in the way of addition, suppression or alteration could have been made without controversy having arisen. Of that there is little trace. 'Othman offended the more religious among the Moslems, and ultimately became very unpopular. But among the charges laid against him, that of having mutilated or altered the Qur'ān is not generally included, and was never made a main point against him. The Shī'ah, it is true, has always held that the Qur'ān was mutilated by the suppression of much which referred to 'Alī and the Prophet's family. But this charge is directed not specially against 'Othman, but equally against the first two caliphs, under whose auspices the first collection is assumed to have been made. It is also founded on dogmatic assumptions which hardly appeal to modern criticism. On general grounds, we may conclude that the 'Othmanic revision was honestly carried out, and reproduced, as closely as was possible to the men in charge of it, what Muhammad had delivered. Study of the Qur'ān will, in my opinion, confirm that conclusion.

Modern study of the Qur'ān has not in fact raised any serious question of its authenticity. The style varies, but is almost unmistakable. So clearly does the whole bear the stamp of the Prophet that doubts of its genuineness hardly arise. The authenticity of a few verses has indeed been questioned. The great French scholar Silvestre de Sacy expressed doubts regarding III, 138. This speaks of the possible death of Muhammad, and is the verse said in a well-known tradition to have been quoted by Abū Bakr, when 'Omar refused to believe the report of the death of the Prophet, which actually had occurred. Weil[1] extended

[1] G. Weil, *Einleitung in den Koran*, 2nd ed., p. 52.

these doubts to a number of other passages which imply the mortality of the Prophet: III, 182, XXI, 36 f., XXIX, 57, XXXIX, 31. Abū Bakr, however, is hardly likely to have invented III, 138 for the occasion; nor does the fact that 'Omar and others professed never to have heard such a verse, weigh very much. The complete Qur'ān was not circulating among Muhammad's followers in written form for them to study, and a verse once delivered may easily have been forgotten in the course of years, even by one who happened to hear it. If the verse does not fit quite smoothly into the context, that is because it is a substitution for the one which follows, as the recurrence of the same rhyme-phrase shows. It fits admirably into the historical situation, for it is a reference, put into an address delivered before Uḥud and re-delivered after the defeat, to the report which had spread during the battle and had no doubt contributed to the rout, that Muhammad had been killed. There is no reason to question the authenticity of a verse so suited to the circumstances.

As for the other verses which imply the mortality of the Prophet, as Schwally[1] points out, they fit well into their contexts and are quite in accord with Muhammad's thought. The humanity and mortality of the Prophet was part of the controversy between him and his opponents, and to take that out of the Qur'ān would be to remove some of its most characteristic portions.

Weil[2] also questioned the authenticity of the famous verse XVII, 1, in which reference is made to the night journey to Jerusalem. His arguments are that there are no other references to such a night journey in the Qur'ān, that it is contrary to Muhammad's usual claim to be simply a messenger and not a wonder-worker, that so far as there is any basis for the later legend in Muhammad's life, it is merely a dream or vision, and that the verse has no connection with what follows. As matters of fact these arguments are correct; but they hardly bear the inference based on them. If we take the verse by itself, without the structure of later legend built upon it, there is nothing in it very much out of keeping

[1] N-S., II, p. 82. [2] Op. cit. p. 74.

with Muhammad's other claims; and there are so many other unconnected verses in the Qur'ān that we can hardly make that an argument against this one in particular.

Finally, Weil [1] questioned XLVI, 14 on the ground that Tradition makes it refer to Abū Bakr, and that presumably it was invented in his honour. But no one who knows the traditional exegesis of the Qur'ān will lay much stress on a reference of that kind. It is full of guesses as to the particular person to whom a verse refers. This particular verse is quite general, and simply develops an injunction several times repeated in the Qur'ān.

Hirschfeld [2] has also questioned the authenticity of certain other verses, in which the name Muhammad occurs, on the ground that this was not the Prophet's real name but was bestowed upon him later. There may be something suspicious in such a name, meaning 'Praised', being borne by the Prophet; but even if it were an assumed name, it might have been adopted in his own life-time. It occurs, not only in the Qur'ān, but in documents handed down by Tradition, the constitution of Medinah, and the treaty of Ḥudaibiyah; in the last the Quraish are said to have objected to the title *rasūl Allāh*, and to *ar-Raḥmān* as a name of God, but raised no question about the name Muhammad. Further, though it does not appear to have been common, there is evidence that Muhammad was in use as a proper name before the time of the Prophet. There is therefore no real reason to doubt that it was his real name.

The most serious attack upon the reliability of the book and the good faith of the collectors was that made by the French scholar, Casanova, in his book, *Mohammed et la fin du monde*, published 1911–1924. His thesis is a development of the view that Muhammad was moved to undertake his mission by the impression made on him by the idea of the approaching Judgment. Casanova thinks that he must have come under the influence of some Christian sect which laid great stress on the near approach of the end of the world.

[1] Op. cit. p. 76.

[2] Hirschfeld, *New Researches into the Composition and Exegesis of the Qur'ār* ,p. 138 ff.

That formed the main theme of his early deliverances and an essential part of his message from beginning to end of his prophetic activity. As the event, however, did not substantiate his prophecy, the leaders of early Islam so manipulated the Qur'ān as to remove that doctrine from it, or at least conceal its prominence. This thesis has not found much acceptance, and it is unnecessary to refute it in detail. The main objection to it is that it is not founded upon study of the Qur'ān so much as upon investigation of some of the byways of early Islam. From this point of view, the book still has value. But when Casanova deals with the Qur'ān itself, his statements often display incorrect exegesis and a total lack of appreciation for the historical development of Muhammad's teaching. As to his main thesis, it is perfectly true that Muhammad proclaimed the coming Judgment and the end of the world. It is true that sometimes he hinted that it might be near; see, for example, XXI, 1, XXVII, 73 f. In other passages he disclaims knowledge of times, and there are great differences in the urgency with which he proclaims the doctrine in different parts of the Qur'ān. But all this is perfectly natural if we regard Muhammad as a living man, faced by both personal problems and outward difficulties in carrying out a task to which he had set his hand. Casanova's thesis makes little allowance for the changes that must have affected the utterances of a man in Muhammad's position through twenty years of ever-changing circumstances. Our acceptance of the Qur'ān as authentic is based, not on any assumption that it is consistent in all its parts—it is not—but on the fact that, however difficult it may be to understand in detail, it does, on the whole, fit into a real historical experience, and bears the stamp of an elusive, but, in outstanding characteristics, quite intelligible personality.

Is the Qur'ān complete?—If we raise the question whether the Qur'ān, as we have it, contains all that Muhammad delivered, the answer is more difficult. It is difficult to prove a negative; and we cannot be sure that no part of the Qur'ān delivered by Muhammad has been lost. Tradition, in fact, gives a number of verses as belonging to the Qur'ān which do not stand in our present book. These may be found collected and examined in N-S., I, pp. 234 ff. The most famous of them is the " verse of stoning ", a verse in which stoning is prescribed as punishment for persons of mature age guilty of fornication. The caliph ʿOmar is said to have been very positive that this was laid down in the Qur'ān, until he was convinced of the contrary by lack of evidence to support his opinion. The verse does not fit very well into either of the surahs to which Tradition assigns it, XXIV and XXXIII, though the former does deal with fornication, v. 2 f. It must therefore remain doubtful whether it was ever actually delivered, but it is not the sort of thing which we should suspect of having been invented without some basis of fact. Then there is the story, often referred to, that Muhammad on one occasion recognised the pagan deities as subordinate beings whose intercession might be of some avail. Tradition has preserved the passage said to have come in LIII, as originally delivered, after vv. 19, 20. There the goddesses al-Lāt, al-ʿUzzā and al-Manāt are mentioned; then came the two verses: " These are the swans exalted, whose intercession is to be hoped for ", or, according to another reading, " is approved (of Allah) ". It seems almost certain that Muhammad made some such concession, and the fact that at v. 26 this surah passes abruptly to deal with the intercession of angels is a slight confirmation of a previous reference to intercession having occurred in it.

The other verses preserved by Tradition are much more doubtful, and the style of them does not seem to be Qur'ānic. Still, whatever view we take of the collection and compilation of the Qur'ān, the possibility remains that parts of it may have been lost. If, according to Tradition, Zaid in collecting the Qur'ān was dependent on chance writings and human memories, parts may easily have been forgotten. On the other hand, if, as critical study of the surahs has suggested, Muhammad revised his deliverances, and sometimes discarded them in favour of new versions, some of them may have been lost altogether. Some things in the Qur'ān seem to be there by accident; others may have disappeared. There is no reason, however, to assume that anything of importance has gone astray; one has rather the impression that pieces which were never meant to be preserved have found their way into the book as finally fixed. The fact that varying, and sometimes even contradictory, deliverances have been preserved, is strong proof that there was no deliberate suppression, and that the editors acted in good faith

NOTE ON THE TEXT OF THE QUR'ĀN

As it is not intended in this volume to deal with textual criticism of the Qur'ān, it may be convenient here to insert a short note on the subject. In the East the tendency has naturally always been to obtain a uniform reading of the text. The ʻOthmanic revision was, as we have seen, an attempt to arrive at that. But that did not prevent a mass of variant readings arising. Not only did the wide extension of Islam favour the prevalence of variants in different districts, but in the early days scholars seem to have exercised considerable freedom, in regard at least to the vocalisation and punctuation of the text. The recognition of the seven ways of reading the text was an attempt to regulate this freedom. It is attributed to the influence of Ibn Mujāhid, a scholar who died in A.H. 324. Accepting the saying attributed to the Prophet that the Qur'ān was revealed in seven readings, he selected seven readers representing the systems prevailing in various districts, one each from Medinah, Meccah, Syria and Baṣrah, and three from Kūfah, whose readings were to be attested by two recorders.

The recognised systems were thus:

Medinah,	that of	Nāfiʻ (d. 169),	recorded by	Warsh (d. 197)
			,,	Qālūn (d. 220)
Meccah,	,,	Ibn Kathīr (d. 120),	recorded by	Bazzī (d. 270)
			,,	Qunbul (d. 291)
Syria,	,,	Ibn ʻĀmir (d. 118),	recorded by	Hishām (d. 245)
			,,	Ibn Dakhwān (d. 242)
Baṣrah,	,,	Abū ʻAmr (d. 154),	recorded by	Dūrī (d. 250)
			,,	Sūsī (d. 261)
Kūfah,	,,	ʻĀsim (d. 128),	recorded by	Ḥafṣ (d. 190)
			,,	Abū Bakr (d. 194)
Kūfah,	,,	Ḥamzah (d. 158),	recorded by	Khalaf (d. 229)
			,,	Khallād (d. 220)
Kūfah,	,,	Kisā'ī (d. 189),	recorded by	Dūrī (d. 250)
			,,	Ḥārith (d. 240)

These seven systems of reading are all recognised as orthodox in Islam, and scholars have prided themselves on knowing the Qur'ān according to all the seven, though each part of the Moslem world preferred one or other of them. Naturally Islam has felt the existence of these varying readings an inconvenience in a sacred book; and we can trace a tendency for one type of text to displace others even in their own districts. To-day the Kūfan reading of 'Āsim recorded by Ḥafṣ stands almost alone, and, as the one adopted in the official Egyptian printed edition, tends to be adopted everywhere.

In the West it is only fairly recently that the study of the Qur'ān text has been taken up systematically. It is generally agreed that the seven orthodox systems of reading are based on the 'Othmanic recension. The variants hardly ever affect the consonantal outline of the text. They give the impression of being largely attempts by exegetes to smooth out the grammar, and throw practically no light upon the condition of the text before the 'Othmanic revision. In the early literature of Islam, however, we find other readings recorded which do not belong to any of the seven recognised systems. These are said to be *shādhdh*, that is, 'peculiar'. Quite a number of these do affect the consonantal text, some of them very considerably, substituting different words or phrases, or even making additions or omissions. The question is whether these go back to early codices which may have been in existence before the revision under 'Othman. If we accept what Tradition says as to the delivery of the Qur'ān and its being memorised or written down by various people, it is reasonable to suppose that very considerable variations existed in the early days. The first task of scholars is to seek out and make accessible early works on the reading of the Qur'ān, and to collect the *shādhdh* readings which have survived. Bergstraesser devoted much labour to this, and his work was carried on by Pretzl. Their conclusions are given in the third volume of the revision of Noeldeke's *Geschichte des Korans*. Professor Arthur Jeffery's book, *Materials for the History of the Qur'ān Text*, gives a large collection of the variants ascribed to the old codices. These collections go a long way to prove that actual written codices did exist before 'Othman's time, and that they had in some respects an independent text. That they preserved a better text is, however, very much open to question.

CHAPTER III

THE FORM OF THE QUR'ĀN

DIVISIONS

LET us now turn to the book itself. It will be convenient to begin with its external form.

Names.—The most usual name for the book is *al-Qur'ān* (Koran, Coran). Though now generally applied to the book as a whole, the word *qur'ān* is used in the book itself in various senses which we shall have to discuss later. The name *al-Furqān*, which from its use in III, 2 is sometimes used instead of *al-Qur'ān*, will also have to be dealt with at a later stage. Another term often applied to the book is *at-Tanzīl*, 'the Revelation', from the Arabic verb *nazzala* 'to send down', used in the Qur'ān in the sense of 'to send down from God', that is, 'to reveal'.

Divisions.—(a) *Ritual Divisions.* In total length the Qur'ān is comparable to the New Testament. For purposes of recitation, the Moslems divide it into thirty approximately equal portions, *juz'*, plural *ajzā'*, corresponding to the number of the days in the month of fasting, Ramaḍān These are usually marked on the margin of copies. Sometimes these are further subdivided into sixty *aḥzāb*, singular *ḥizb*, two to each *juz'*, and these again into quarters, *rub' al-ḥizb*, which may also be marked on the margin. There is also a division into *manāzil*, singular *manzil*, to facilitate the recital of the Qur'ān in the course of a week. These are external divisions which take little or no account of the natural sections of the book, and do not really concern us here.

(b) *Surahs.* These, on the contrary, are real divisions in the body of the book. The nearest equivalent is perhaps 'chapter'. The word *sūrah*, plural *suwar*, also occurs in the text, and its derivation is doubtful. The most accepted view is that it comes from the Hebrew *shūrāh*, 'a row', used of bricks in a wall, vines, etc. From this the sense of a series of passages, or chapter, may perhaps be deduced, but it is rather forced. Besides, it hardly gives the sense in which the word is used in the Qur'ān itself. In X, 39 the challenge is issued: "Do they say: 'He has devised it?'; let them come then with a surah like it". In XI, 16 the challenge is to bring ten surahs like those which have been produced. But in XXVIII, 49, where a similar challenge is given, it is to produce a book, or writing, from Allah. Evidently the sense required is something like 'revelation' or 'Scripture'. I have therefore suggested that the word is derived from the Syriac *ṣūrṭā*, which has the sense of 'writing', 'text of Scripture', and even 'the Scriptures'. The laws which govern the interchange of consonants in Arabic and Syriac are against that derivation, but in Syriac itself the spelling of the word varies to *ṣūrthā*, and even *sūrthā*; and in any case, in words directly borrowed, these philological laws do not necessarily hold.

The surahs number 114. The first, known as the *Fātiḥah*, 'the Opening', is a short prayer, very much used in Islam. The two last are short charms which, as already noted, Ibn Mas'ūd seems not to have included in his collection of the Qur'ān. The rest are arranged roughly in the order of length, which varies from many pages to a line or two. Thus II, the longest, occupies, in Redslob's edition of Fluegel's text, 37 pages of 19 lines each, plus nearly 12 lines, while several near the end occupy 2 lines or less, CVIII, CXII. How far this arrangement goes back to Muhammad himself, and how far it is due to the compilers, we shall probably never be able to unravel completely; but we shall probably see reason in what follows for holding that he had more to do with it than the traditional account allows.

Headings of Surahs.—The surahs are marked off from each other by the occurrence of headings. These are of set form. First comes the name or title of the surah. That is the name by which the surah is usually referred to by Oriental scholars, instead of the number generally used in the West. It has, as a rule, no reference to the subject-matter of the surah, but is simply taken from some prominent, or unusual word in the surah. Usually this word will occur near the beginning, but this is not always so. Thus XVI is entitled " The Bee ", but the bee is not mentioned in it until v. 70, more than half-way through ; it is, however, the only passage in which the bee is mentioned in the Qur'ān. Again, XXVI is entitled " The Poets " ; but the only mention of the poets is in v. 224 ff., at the very end of the surah. But again, that is the only passage in the Qur'ān which refers to the poets—apart from those in which the suggestion that the Prophet is himself a poet is indignantly rejected. And the passage is rather a striking one ; probably no Arab who heard that brief, but trenchant, description of his much-belauded poets would forget it. There seems to be no rule in this matter ; the title is simply taken from some word in the surah sufficiently striking to serve as a means of identification. (We may compare the reference in the Gospels, Mark xii, 26, Luke xx, 37, to Exodus iii, as " The Bush "). Sometimes a surah has two such titles, both being still in use ; for example, IX, XL, XLI ; and we find references in early Islamic literature to a few other titles in use at one time but later dropped. That supports the assumption that these titles do not belong to the Qur'ān proper, but have been introduced by later scholars and editors for convenience of reference. To this later scholarly apparatus also evidently belongs the statement of dates and of the number of verses contained in the surah, which follows the title. The dating does not go beyond the bare description of the surah as Meccan, or Medinan ; nor are these descriptions to be understood as necessarily applying to the surah as a whole. Moslem scholars have always been quite open to admit that surahs are composite, and that one marked as Meccan may contain one or more Medinan passages, and vice versa. These indications are to be regarded merely as the judgments of the compilers, or early scholars, as to the period at which the main basis or content of each surah was produced. The modern Egyptian printed edition specifies the verses which are exceptions, and also indicates the position of the surah in order of delivery.

Following the number of verses comes the *bismillah*. At

the head of all the surahs, except one, stands the phrase, *bi-smi llāhi r-raḥmāni r-raḥīm*, " In the name of God, the Merciful, the Compassionate ". The exception is IX. Moslem commentators say that the omission is due to this surah having been revealed shortly before Muhammad's death, so that he left no instructions on the matter. That cannot be correct, but it implies that in the view of Moslem scholars it was Muhammad himself who was responsible for the placing of the *bismillah* at the head of the surahs. That it belongs to the composition rather than to the editing of the surahs is confirmed by the fact that in XXVII, where Solomon is represented as inditing a letter to the Queen of Sheba, the letter begins with the *bismillah*, as if that were the appropriate heading for a document coming from a prophet. So also in XCVI, Muhammad is commanded to recite in the name of his Lord. It has been suggested that the omission of the phrase at the head of IX may be due to VIII and IX having originally formed one surah. VIII is short for its position; on the other hand VIII and IX together would make a surah much too long for its position. The real reason is that surah IX begins with a proclamation which is already sufficiently attested as being issued in the name of Allah. The *bismillah* was therefore superfluous. The exception thus confirms the conclusion that the *bismillah* is not a mere editorial formula, but forms the heading of the surah as it was composed. That need not, of course, be taken so strictly as to exclude the possibility of its having in some cases been added by the compilers or editors.

Mysterious Letters.—Following the *bismillah* at the beginning of 29 surahs stands a letter, or a group of letters, which are simply read as separate letters of the alphabet. These letters are one of the mysteries of the Qur'ān. No satisfactory explanation of their meaning, if they have one, has ever been given, nor has any convincing reason been found for their having been placed where they stand. If reference be made to the table given at the end of this chapter, it will be seen that some occur once only, singly or in combination, and before isolated surahs, but that there are other combinations which occur before several surahs, and that the surahs having the same combination of letters stand in groups. Thus the *ḥawāmīm*, as they are called, that is, the surahs in front of which the letters *ḥā'*, *mīm* stand, if we include the one in which these letters are combined with others, form a solid block, XL-XLVI The surahs with *alif*, *lām*, *rā'*, including XIII which has *mīm* in addition, form a block X-XV. The *ṭā'*, *sīn*, and *ṭā'*, *sīn*, *mīm* surahs form another little group XXVI-XXVIII. The *alif*, *lām*, *mīm* surahs are separated; II and III stand together, VII, which has *ṣād* in addition, stands by itself, XIII is included in the *alif*, *lām*, *rā'* group, and then there is the block XXIX-XXXII. Altogether we get the impression of groups of surahs, similarly marked, which have been kept together when the Qur'ān was put in its present shape.

Consideration of the lengths of the surahs tends to confirm this. A glance at the table will show that on the whole the surahs stand in order of decreasing length, and this almost looks like the principle on which the order of the surahs has been arranged. It is equally evident that there are many deviations from the strict sequence, and it is necessary to guard against laying too much stress on a mechanical rule of this kind, which is not likely to have been carefully carried through. But some of the deviations from the rule of decreasing length seem to be connected with these groups of surahs. Thus, if we take the group XL-XLVI, we find that the first is a little longer than XXXIX, while XLV, and especially XLIV, are short for their position. It looks as if the order of decreasing length had been departed from in order to keep the *ḥawāmīm* group as it stood before the final arrangement was undertaken. Again, taking the *alif*, *lām*, *rā'* group, we find that X, XI, XII stand approximately in their proper position according to length, but XIII, XIV, XV are short, and with XVI we return again to something like the length of X. It looks as if this group had been inserted as a solid block. On the other hand, the *alif*, *lām*, *mīm* surahs are placed in different positions, II and III, the longest surahs, at the very beginning, XXIX-XXXII in a group much farther on, as if the deviation from the rule would have been too great, and the group had therefore been broken up. These facts give some support to the supposition that, when the present order of the surahs was fixed, the groups marked by these mysterious letters were already in existence.

That, of course, throws no light on the meaning of these symbols. But founding on this assumption and on the tradition as to Zaid b. Thābit's collection of the Qur'ān after Muhammad's death, some European scholars have regarded these letters as abbreviations of the names of persons who had previously, for their own use, collected, memorised, or written down certain surahs, and from whom, then, Zaid obtained them. Thus the *ḥawāmīm* would have been obtained from somebody whose name was abbreviated to *ḥā' mīm*; and so on. It seems a plausible theory; but the difficulty is to suggest names of possible persons who might be so indicated. No one has satisfactorily solved that problem. Hirschfeld, for instance, who tried to work it out, takes *ṣād* as denoting Ḥafṣah, *kāf*, Abū Bakr, *nūn*, 'Othman. Again, it is difficult to see why, for important surahs like II and III, the collectors should have been dependent apparently upon one person, denoted by *alif*, *lām*, *mīm*, whom Hirschfeld takes to be al-Mughīrah; while other much less important surahs had no letters at their head, and were thus presumably general property.

Much the same difficulty attaches to the suggestion of Goossens (*Der Islam*, 1923) that these letters are contractions for disused titles of the surahs. It may quite well be that a title which had acquired some wide usage, but was not finally adopted, was retained in an abbreviated form. But, if so, it is necessary to find some word or phrase in the surah for which the letters at the head of it may be accepted as a contraction. Goossens succeeded in a number of cases, but in some his solutions were impossible, and in others he had to assume some drastic rearrangement of contents and change of division of surahs. Further, he did not succeed very well in explaining why several surahs should have had the same title, as the groups with the same letters at their head would imply.

These suggestions go on the assumption that the letters belong to the collection and redaction of the Qur'ān, and are therefore later than the texts before which they stand. Nor does it make any real difference if we suppose them to have been marks used by Muhammad or his scribes to identify or classify the surahs. These letters always follow the *bismillah*, and we have seen reason to think that the *bismillah* belongs to the text and not to the editing. It seems probable, therefore, that these letters also belong to the composition of the text, and were not external marks added either in Muhammad's life-time or by later compilers. That is the view of all Oriental interpreters. They generally try to find some meaning in the symbols. But there is no agreement amongst them as to the exact sense, and their attempts to find in them contractions of words or phrases are just as arbitrary as those of European scholars.

Noeldeke, to whom the suggestion that these letters were indications of names of collectors was originally due, in some of his later articles departed from it, and adopted the view that they were simply meaningless symbols, perhaps magic signs, or imitations of the writing of the heavenly Book which was being conveyed to Muhammad. That they have something to do with the revelation is confirmed by the fact that the majority of the surahs at the head of which they stand begin with some reference to the Book, the Qur'ān or the revelation. Of the 29 surahs to which they are prefixed only three, XIX, XXIX and XXX, have no such reference immediately following. Considering how often the Book is referred to later in it, XIX can hardly be counted an exception. Analysis also shows that surahs marked by such letters are of either late Meccan or Medinan composition, or at least have traces of late revision ; they belong to the time when Muhammad was consciously producing a revelation similar to the revelation in the hands of previous monotheists. It is possible that he may have tried to imitate some of the writing in which these scriptures existed. In fact, in some of these combinations of letters it seems possible to see words written in Syriac or Hebrew, which have been afterwards read as Arabic. That suggestion, however, like others, seems impossible to carry through. We end where we began ; the letters are mysterious, and have so far baffled interpretation.

(c) *Verses.* The surahs are divided into verses, which are termed *'āyāt*, singular *'āyah*. This word is also used in the text. It is, however, only in later passages, if at all, that it has the sense of ' verses '. It is much more commonly used in the sense of ' sign ', ' wonder ' It is related to the Hebrew *'ōth*, and ' sign ' is evidently its basic meaning. The verse-division is not artificially imposed, as the verse-divisions of the Christian Bible frequently are. It belongs to the composition of the Qur'ān, and the verses are distinctly marked by the occurrence of rhyme, or, more strictly, assonance. Differences in the division into verses, and consequently differences in the numbering of the verses, do occur in the various readings, or recensions, of the Qur'ān; and, unfortunately, the verse-numbering of Fluegel's edition, which is the one generally used in the West, does not exactly correspond to that most generally adopted in the East, or in fact to that of any of the Oriental recensions. That is due to the occurrence of cases in which it can be doubted whether the rhyme was intended, or simply came in accidentally, and that again depends on the nature of the rhymes, or assonances, which are largely produced by the use of the same grammatical forms or terminations (see p. 67). But a very cursory examination of the Qur'ān in the original Arabic will serve to convince anyone that the verses were intended to rhyme.

The length of the verses, like the length of the surahs, varies much. In some surahs, and these generally the longer ones, the verses are long and trailing; in others, especially the shorter ones near the end of the book, the verses are short and crisp. That, however, is not an invariable rule. Surah XCVIII, which is comparatively short, consists of 8 fairly long verses; XXVI, which is fairly long, has over 200 verses mostly quite short. But it may be noted that, as a rule, the verses in the same surah, or, at least, in the same passage or part of a surah, are of approximately the same length. There are exceptions even to that generalisation, but on the whole it remains valid, particularly where the verses are short.

The verses are in prose, without metre, though in some

passages, for example LXXIV, 1-7, XCI, 1-10, there is a kind of rhythm or metre of stresses. That feature is due rather to the shortness of the rhyming verses and the repetition of the same form of phrase, than to any effort to carry through a strict metrical form. Where the verses are of any length, and the form of phrase varies, no fixed metre, either of syllables or of stresses, can be traced. The Qur'ān is written in rhymed prose, in verses without metre or definitely fixed length, their ends marked by the occurrence of a rhyme, or assonance, which, as a rule, remains the same throughout a passage.

THE DRAMATIC FORM

We have seen that Muhammad believed himself to be inspired and that his messages came to him by prompting from without. On the whole he drew a clear distinction between what came to him in this way and his own thoughts and sayings. The Qur'ān, therefore, is not cast in the form of his own words to his fellow-men. Only in a very few passages does Muhammad speak in his own person; in XXVII, 93 ff. we have one of those declarations of his position which are usually preceded by the word "say", left, perhaps by inadvertence, without that prefix. Whether XXVI, 221 ff. are in Muhammad's own words is uncertain, though that would be the most natural assumption. There are other passages in regard to which we may be doubtful, for example, LXXXI, 15 ff., LXXXIV, 16-19, XCII, 14 ff. Some of the lists of 'signs' adduced as evidence of Allah's power might be regarded as being in the messenger's own words; so also descriptions of the Last Day like XCI, 1-10. Many passages in later surahs are directly addressed to the people, and speak of Allah in the third person, as if they were spoken by Muhammad himself; but we find frequent indications that the dramatic setting is different (see p. 62). We must therefore be chary of assuming that passages in the Qur'ān are in Muhammad's own words, though one can hardly avoid the impression that some of the early pieces are in that form.

It is usually assumed, in accordance with Moslem doctrine, that the speaker is Allah, and that the Prophet is addressed as the recipient of the revelation. This corresponds to the setting in many passages. Allah speaks sometimes in the first person singular. A passage like XCII, 14 ff. is doubtful, but LI, 56 f., " I have not created jinn and men but that they should serve Me; I desire not any provision from them, nor do I desire that they should feed Me ", is clearly cast in the words of Allah. So in LXVII, 18, LXXIV, 11-15, and even in such distinctly Medinan passages as II, 38, 44 (where Allah makes, as it were, a personal appeal to the Children of Israel) and II, 182. Much more frequently, however, we find the first person plural used where Allah is without doubt the speaker. As creation is, in the doctrine of the Qur'ān, the prerogative of Allah, passages in which the speaker claims to have created may be taken as certainly spoken by Allah; thus XV, 26 f., XVII, 72, XXI, 16 f., XXIII, 12-14, and many other passages. If we take passages in which creation is not mentioned but which are in the same form, we shall find that a great deal of the Qur'ān is thus placed in the mouth of Allah speaking in the plural of majesty.

It is also clear in many passages that the Prophet is being addressed. The well-known verses, so often cited as the earliest revelations, LXXIV, 1 ff., " O thou clothed in the *dithār*, arise and warn, thy Lord magnify . . ." and XCVI, 1 ff., " Recite in the name of thy Lord . . ." are evidently addressed to the Prophet. The use of the second person singular is very common in the Qur'ān, the words being thus addressed to a single individual, who is no doubt Muhammad himself. Many passages are indeed personal to the Prophet: encouragements, exhortations, assurances of the reality of his inspiration, rebukes, pieces of advice as to how to act. On the other hand, many passages thus addressed to the Prophet have no special reference to him but contain matter of interest to others as well. That is, in fact, quite frequently stated, in such phrases as: " Surely in that is a lesson for those who fear ". Even when not stated, it is the evident intention that the communication should be made public; the Prophet is exhorted to 'recite', and that was no doubt the method by which these revelations were made known to the people. Sometimes the Prophet is addressed as the representative of the people, and after a direct address to him the passage may continue with the second person plural, as in LXV, 1 ff.

But the assumption that Allah is Himself the speaker in all these passages leads to difficulties. For in a great many of them we find Allah being referred to in the third person. It is no doubt allowable for a speaker to refer to himself in the third person occasionally, but the extent to which we find the Prophet apparently being addressed and told about Allah as a third person, arouses suspicion. It has, in fact, been made a matter of ridicule that, in the Qur'ān Allah is made to swear by Himself. That He uses oaths in some of the passages beginning, "I swear not . . .", for example in LXXV, 1 ff., XC, 1 ff., can hardly be denied. This was probably a traditional formula. But "By thy Lord" is difficult in the mouth of Allah. "Thy Lord" is, in fact, a very common designation of Allah in the Qur'ān, as in the two early passages above quoted. Now, there is one passage which everyone acknowledges to be spoken by angels, namely XIX, 65 f.: "We come not down but by command of thy Lord; to Him belongs what is before us and what is behind us and what is between that; nor is thy Lord forgetful, Lord of the heavens and the earth and what is between them; so serve Him, and endure patiently in His service; knowest thou to Him a namesake?" In XXXVII, 161-166 it is almost equally clear that angels are the speakers. This, once admitted, may be extended to passages in which it is not so clear. In fact, difficulties in many passages are removed by interpreting the "We" as angels rather than as Allah Himself speaking in the plural of majesty. It is not always easy to distinguish between the two, and nice questions sometimes arise in places where there is a sudden change from Allah being spoken of in the third person to "We" claiming to do things usually ascribed to Allah. Have VI, 99 and XXV, 47 ff., for example, been somewhat hurriedly revised, or have the angels, in Muhammad's ideas, assumed other functions of Providence, besides the communication of revelations ?

In the later portions of the Qur'ān, it seems to be an almost invariable rule that the words are addressed by the angels, or by Gabriel using the plural " We ", to the Prophet, Allah being spoken of in the third person, and His will and commands being thus communicated to men. This is the case even where the people or the believers are directly addressed. In some of these passages one might assume that Muhammad was addressing his followers in his own words. But in so many of them there are clear indications that the angel speaks that we must assume that that is the form in them all. Muhammad has, in fact, reached assurance in his position, and hence in his form. He is the mouthpiece of the divine will, which is communicated to him by Gabriel, and thus, like a confidential official, he stands on the border-line between the king's court and the subjects. Subject he is always. Sometimes he receives messages to convey to the people, or he receives commands and exhortations intended for them ; sometimes he is directly addressed as the representative of the people ; at other times special exhortations and directions for his own conduct are addressed to him ; at times he steps, as it were, across the line, and facing round upon the people conveys the divine commands and exhortations direct to them. But in these late passages the dramatic setting remains fairly consistent : Allah is a third person in the background, the " We " of the speaker is the angel (or angels), the messages are addressed to the Prophet, even where the people are directly addressed the words come through him but he is mouthpiece only. In earlier parts of the Qur'ān, however, the dramatic setting varies to some extent, as has been said above, and this often gives an indication of a break in the composition.[1]

[1] Direct address is found in the following passages :

(*a*) O ye people : II, 19b-20, 163-164, 167-169, IV, 1, 168, 174, X, 23-26, 58, XXII, 1-4, 5-8, 72, XXXI, 32-34, XXXV, 3, 5, 16, XLIX, 13.

(*b*) O ye who have believed : II, 98, 148, 173, 179, 204 f., 255, 266-267, 269 f., 278-281, 282 f., III, 95, 97 f., 114-116, 125-128, 150, 200, IV, 23-25, 33-35, 46, 62, 73-78, 96, 134, 135 f., 143, V, 1, 2, 8, 11, 14, 39-41, 56-58, 59-61, 62-63, 89-90, 95, 96, 101, 104, 105-107, VIII, 15, 20-23, 24-26, 27 f., 29, 47-48,

TABLE OF THE SURAHS OF THE QUR'ĀN IN NUMERICAL ORDER

Giving the number of verses, and the lengths as shown by the pages and lines occupied in Redslob's edition of Fluegel's text; also the initial letters where these occur; for convenience *alif* is here indicated by A. The *bismillah* in this edition occupies a full line, which has been counted.

No.	*Initial Letters*	*Verses*	*Pages*	*Lines*
1		7		6
2	ALM	286	37½ +	815½
3	ALM	200	21½ +	409½
4		175	23½ –	445½
5		120	17½	332½
6		165	19 –	358½
7	ALMṢ	205	21 –	398½
8		76	8 –	149½
9		130	16 –	301½
10	ALR	109	11½ –	215½
11	ALR	123	11½	221
12	ALR	111	11	209½
13	ALMR	43	5 +	99
14	ALR	52	5 +	99½
15	ALR	99	4½	85
16		128	11½	217
17		111	10	195
18		110	10 –	184½
19	KHY'Ṣ	98	6	114½
20	ṬH	135	8½	159
21		112	7½	145
22		78	8 –	150

IX, 23, 28, 34-35, 38 ff., 120, 124, XXII, 76, XXIV, 21, 27-29, 57-60, XXXIII, 9-27, 41-43, 48, 53 f., 56-58, 69-71, XLVII, 8-12, 35-40, XLIX, 1, 2 f., 6-8, 11, 12, LVII, 28 f., LVIII, 10, 12, 13 f., LIX, 18, LX, 1-3, 10 f., 13, LXI, 2-4, 10-12, 14, LXIII, 9-11, LXIV, 14-18, LXV, 11-12, LXVI, 6 f., 8. Cf. XXIX, 56-58.

(*c*) O thou messenger: V, 45-47, 71.
O thou prophet: VIII, 65, 66 f., IX, 74 f., XXXIII, 1-3, 28 ff., 44, 49-52, 59, LX, 12, LXV, 1-7, LXVI, 1 f., 9.
O thou heavily burdened: LXXIII, 1 ff.
O thou clothed in the *dithār*: LXXIV, 1 ff.

(*d*) O Children of Israel: II, 38 f., 44 f., 46-58, 116 f., 118 ff., XX, 82-84.
O People of the Book: III, 58 ff., 63, 64, IV, 169, V, 18, 22.

No.	*Initial Letters*	*Verses*	*Pages*	*Lines*
23		118	7 −	129½
24		64	8½	159
25		77	5½	109
26	ṬSM	228	9 −	169½
27	ṬS	95	7 +	137½
28	ṬSM	88	9 −	168½
29	ALM	69	6 +	120½
30	ALM	60	5 +	99
31	ALM	34	3 +	62½
32	ALM	30	2½	46½
33		73	8½	158½
34		54	5½	102
35		45	5 +	98
36	YS	83	5 −	90
37		182	6 +	118
38	Ṣ	88	5 −	90
39		75	7½	140
40	ḤM	85	7½	145
41	ḤM	54	5 −	94
42	ḤM'SQ	53	5 +	100
43	ḤM	89	5½	104
44	ḤM	59	2½	46½
45	ḤM	36	3 +	59
46	ḤM	35	4 −	75
47		40	3½	67½
48		29	3½	69
49		18	2 +	42½
50	Q	45	2½	46½
51		60	2½	46½
52		49	2 +	40
53		62	2½	44
54		55	2½	44½
55		78	2½	50
56		96	3 −	54½
57		29	3½	70½
58		22	3	57
59		24	3 −	54½
60		13	2½	43½
61		14	1½	28
62		11	1 +	22

No.	*Initial Letters*	*Verses*	*Pages*	*Lines*
63		11	1 +	23
64		18	1½	31
65		12	2 –	35
66		12	1½	31
67		30	2 +	40
68	N	52	2 +	40
69		52	2 –	35
70		44	1½	30½
71		29	1½	28½
72		28	2 –	34
73		20	1½	25
74		55	1½	33½
75		40	1 +	22
76		31	1½	32½
77		50	1½	27
78		41	1½	24½
79		46	1½	25½
80		42	1	19
81		29	1 –	15
82		19	½	11½
83		36	1½	25½
84		25	1 –	15
85		22	1 –	15½
86		17	½	9
87		19	½	10½
88		26	½	13½
89		30	1 –	18½
90		20	½	11½
91		15	½	8½
92		21	½	11
93		11	½	6
94		8		4½
95		8	½	6
96		19	½	10½
97		5		4½
98		8	½	12½
99		8	½	6
100		11	½	6½
101		8	½	6
102		8		5

No.	*Initial Letters*	*Verses*	*Pages*	*Lines*
103		3		3
104		9		5
105		5		4
106		4		$3\frac{1}{2}$
107		7		$4\frac{1}{2}$
108		3		$2\frac{1}{2}$
109		6		4
110		3		$3\frac{1}{2}$
111		5		$3\frac{1}{2}$
112		4		$2\frac{1}{2}$
113		5		$3\frac{1}{2}$
114		6		$3\frac{1}{2}$

CHAPTER IV

THE STRUCTURE AND STYLE OF THE QUR'ĀN

Rhymes.—The Qur'ān, then, presents itself in the form of surahs divided into verses. The questions arise whether the surahs are unities, and, if so, whether they show any organic structure ; or, if they are not unities, whether we can discern how they have been built up. In approaching these questions, if we follow the method of starting from externals, it will be well to be clear as to the nature of the rhyme which marks the close of verses.

There is no attempt in the Qur'ān to produce the strict rhyme of poetry. In an Arabic poem each verse had to end in the same rhyme-consonant surrounded by the same vowels—an interchange of *i* and *u* was allowed, though considered a weakness. Short inflectional vowels following the rhyme-consonant were usually retained, and, if retained, were pronounced long at the end of the line. Only in very exceptional cases is it possible to find this type of rhyme in the Qur'ān. What we find is, rather, assonance, in which short inflectional vowels at the end of a verse are disregarded, and for the rest, the vowels, particularly their length, and the fall of the accent, that is the form of the end-word of the verse, are of more importance than the consonants. Of course the consonant may remain the same, but that is not essential. Thus in CXII the four verses rhyme in *-ad*, if we disregard the inflections ; in CV we have the rhyme in *-īl*, if we disregard end-vowels and allow *ū* in place of *ī* in the last verse. In CIII *r* is rhyme-consonant, but the inflections vary and have to be disregarded, though, for pronunciation, we require a short vowel sound of some kind after the *r*, or, alternatively, a short vowel before it which is not in the form. In LIV, where *r* as rhyme-consonant is carried through

55 verses, we have not only to disregard the end-vowels but to accept variations of the preceding vowel, *i* and *u* and even *a* occurring in that position; the assonance is *-fa'il*, that is, an open syllable with short vowel which takes the accent, followed by a syllable with short vowel closed by *r* which thus becomes a rhyme-consonant. On the other hand, the accusative termination *-an* is often retained, being probably pronounced as *-ā*; for example in XVIII, LXXII and C, where the accusative termination seems to be essential to the rhyme. Further, the feminine termination *-atun* dropped not only its inflections but also its *t* sound; cf. CIV, where, if we drop end-vowels and pronounce the feminine termination as *ā* or *ah*, we get a consistent assonance formed by an accented syllable followed by a short unaccented syllable and the ending, that is *fá'alah*, in which both vowels and consonants are variable, but the place of the accent and the ending *-ah* remain the same. The actual rhyme-words are: *lúmazah*, *'áddadah*, *ákhladah*, *al-ḥúṭamah*, *al-ḥúṭamah*, *al-mū́qadah*, *al-'áf'idah*, *mú'ṣadah*, *mumáddadah*; this illustrates the retention of the same sound formation with variation of consonant, and even of vowel. In XCIX we have a similar assonance, formed by a long accented *ā*, followed by a short syllable, and the feminine suffix *-hā*, that is *-ā́lahā*, the *-hā* being in one verse replaced by the plural suffix *-hum*. The assonance of XLVII is the same, but with greater variation of suffix.

The structure of the Arabic language, in which words fall into definite types of forms, was favourable to the production of such assonances. But even in the short surahs we find a tendency to rely for the assonance on grammatical terminations, for example the suffix *-hā* as in XCIX above, and in XCI assonance *-ī́hā*. In the longer surahs this tendency increases. Thus in LV the assonance depends very largely upon the dual-ending *-ān*. Fairly often in the longer surahs, though hardly ever carried through unbroken, we find the assonance *-ā(l)*, that is, a long *ā* vowel followed by a (variable) consonant; so in parts of II, III, XIV, XXXVIII (almost complete), XXXIX, XL, and sporadically elsewhere. But in the great majority of the surahs of any length, and even in some of the short ones, the prevailing assonance is -*ī*(*l*), that is, a long *ī* or *ū* sound (these interchange freely) followed by a consonant. This depends very largely on the plural endings of nouns and verbs, -*ūn* and -*īn*, varied by words of the form *fa'īl*, one of the commonest forms in Arabic. By far the greater part of the Qur'ān shows this assonance.

With an assonance depending thus upon grammatical endings there may occasionally be doubt as to whether it was really intended. The varying systems of verse-numbering depend to some extent, though not entirely, upon varying judgment as to where the rhyme was intended to fall in particular cases. But that assonance at the end of verses was intended and deliberately sought for can hardly be questioned. In passages with short verses and frequently recurring assonances the intention is unmistakable. But even in surahs in which the verses are long, we find special turns of phrase employed in order to produce the assonance. Thus the preposition *min* with a plural participle is often used where a participle in the singular would have sufficiently given the sense; so that we get phrases like "one of the unbelievers" instead of simply "an unbeliever" because the former gives the rhyming plural-ending, while the latter does not: for example III, 53, 75, VII, 103. *Kānū* with an imperfect or participle in the plural often takes the place of a simple perfect plural; for example in II, 54, VII, 35. Or an imperfect plural may be used where a perfect might have been expected, as in V, 74. Occasionally a phrase is added at the end of a verse which is really otiose as regards sense but supplies the assonance, as in XII, 10, XXI, 68, 79, 104. Sometimes the sense is strained in order to produce the rhyme, for instance in IV, where statements regarding Allah are inappropriately thrown into the past by the use of *kāna* in front of them, the accusative ending on which the rhyme depends being thereby obtained. The form of a proper name is occasionally modified for the sake of rhyme, as *Sīnīn*, XCV, *Ilyāsīn*, XXXVII, 130.

Rhyme-phrases.—Statements regarding Allah occur frequently at the end of verses, especially in the long surahs, where the verses also are of some length. Where the verses are short, the word or phrase which carries the rhyme forms as a rule an integral part of the grammatical structure and is necessary to the sense. But in some passages we find that the phrases which carry the rhyme can be detached without dislocating the structure of what remains, as in XLI, 8 ff. Sometimes, in fact, the rhyme-phrase interrupts the sense, as in VI, 142 ff.; but this is exceptional. Usually the phrase is appropriate enough but stands apart from the rest of the verse. These detachable rhyme-phrases—most of which carry the assonance in *-ī(i)*—tend to be repeated, and to assume a set form which recurs either verbally or with slight changes in wording. Thus *inna fī dhālika la-'āyatan li-l-mu'minīn* often closes the account of a 'sign'. *'Alā llāhi fa-l-yatawakkal il-mu'minūn* (*il-mutawakkilūn*) occurs 9 times. *Wa-llāhu 'alīm ḥakīm* occurs 12 times, or, if we include slight modifications, 18 times. There are other combinations of adjectives referring to Allah which are frequently used in the same way. Perhaps the most frequent of all such phrases is *inna llāha 'alā kulli shai'in qadīr*, "verily Allah over everything hath power", which is used 6 times in II, 4 times in III, 4 times in V and some 18 times in other surahs. To have a stock of such phrases was no doubt a convenience for a busy man who had adopted a rhyming style of utterance. But there is also a certain effectiveness in their use. These sententious phrases regarding Allah are most often used to close a deliverance, and serve at once to press home a truth by repetition and to clinch the authority of what is laid down. They act as a kind of refrain.

Refrains.—The use of actual refrain, in the sense of the same words occurring at more or less regular intervals, is sparse in the Qur'ān. It is anything but effectively used in LV, where the same words "Which then of the benefits of your Lord will ye twain count false?" occur in vv. 12, 15, 18, 21, 23, 25, 28, and from there on in practically each alternate verse, without regard to the sense, which they frequently interrupt. The same tendency to increasing frequency and disregard of sense appears in the use of the words, "Woe that day to those who count false!" as a kind of refrain before sections of surah LXXVII. Didactically effective, on the other hand, is the use of refrain in the groups of stories of former prophets which occur in various surahs. The stories in these groups not only show similarities of wording throughout, but are often closed by the same formula; cf. those in XI, XXVI, XXXVII and LIV.

Internal Rhymes.—In addition to the rhymes which occur at the end of the verses, we can occasionally detect rhymes, different from the end-rhymes, occurring in the middle, or elsewhere, in the verse. These give the impression of a varied arrangement of rhymes. R. Geyer pointed out some of these in an article in the *Göttinger Gelehrte Anzeigen*, 1909, and argued that stanzas with such varied rhymes were sometimes deliberately intended in the Qur'ān. If that were so, we should expect the same form to recur. But in going through Geyer's examples we do not get the impression that any pre-existing forms of stanza were being reproduced, or that any fixed forms of stanza at all were being used. There are no fixed patterns. All that can be said is that in some passages we do find such mixtures of rhymes, just as, quite often, we find, within a surah, breaks in the regular recurring rhyme at the end of the verses. But, as we shall see, these facts are to be otherwise explained.

Strophes.—A similar argument applies to the contention of D. H. Mueller in his book, *Die Propheten in ihrer ursprünglichen Form*, Vienna, 1895. He sought to show that composition in strophes was characteristic of prophetic literature, in the Old Testament as well as in the Qur'ān. From the Qur'ān he adduced many passages which appear to support such a view, for example LVI. But if we are to speak of strophic form, we expect some regularity in the length and arrangement of the strophes. Mueller, however, failed to show that there was any such regularity. What his evidence does show is that many surahs of the Qur'ān fall into short sections or paragraphs. But these are not of fixed length, nor do they seem to follow any pattern of length. Their length is determined not by any consideration of form, but by the subject or incident treated in each.

Short Pieces.—Interpreted in this way, Mueller's contention brings out a real characteristic of Qur'ān style. It is disjointed. Only very seldom do we find in it evidence of sustained unified composition at any great length. The longest such pieces are the addresses found in some of the later surahs. The address before Uḥud has become broken up and is now difficult to unravel from the middle of III. But the address after the Day of the Trench and the overthrow of the Quraiẓah, XXXIII, 9-27, and the assurance to the disappointed Moslems after the truce of Ḥudaibiyah, XLVIII, 18-29, may be taken as examples of fairly lengthy pieces evidently composed for one special purpose. Some of the narratives, too, in the Qur'ān, especially accounts of Moses and of Abraham, run to considerable length. But they tend to fall into separate incidents, instead of being recounted straightforwardly. This is particularly true of the longest of all, the story of Joseph in XII. In other surahs, even where we can trace some connection in thought, this paragraph arrangement is very evident. In LXXX, for instance, we can persuade ourselves that a line of thought governs the collection of the separate pieces, running from the Prophet's dissatisfaction with his cajoling of the wealthy, through the sublimity of the message which ought to commend itself, but is thwarted by man's ingratitude for religious and temporal benefits, up to the description of the final Judgment-day. But one has a stronger impression of the distinctness of the separate pieces than of their unity; and one of them, vv. 24-32, bears evident traces of having been fitted into a context to which it did not originally belong. In the longer surahs devoted largely to political and legal matters we find, as is natural enough, that subjects vary, and, while we do find here and there considerable blocks of legislation devoted to one subject, for example the rules regarding divorce in II, 228 ff., we do not get the impression that an effort has been made to produce a surah dealing systematically with any subject. One surah may contain passages dealing with many different subjects, and the same subject may be treated in several different surahs.

The Qur'ān itself tells us that it was delivered in

separate pieces, XVII, 107, XXV, 34. Neither of these passages tells us anything as to the length of the pieces. But Moslem Tradition, which assigns different 'occasions' to passages consisting of a verse or two, favours the assumption that the pieces were short. We were led to this by consideration of Muhammad's method of composition (pp. 33-35 above). It corresponds to what we actually find in the Qur'ān. Not only are there a considerable number of short pieces standing alone as separate surahs, but the longer surahs contain many short pieces which are complete in themselves, and could be removed without serious derangement of the context. Consideration of the passages introduced by formulae of direct address (pp. 60, 62, 63 above) will show that. II, 173-175, for instance, deals with retaliation; it comes indeed amongst other passages addressed to the believers and dealing with other subjects, but it has no necessary connection with them. V, 14 stands quite by itself, clear enough, if only we knew the event to which it refers, but if it had been absent we should never have suspected that something had fallen out. XLIX, 13 may be quoted as illustrating the form of these passages: "O ye people, We have created you of male and female and made you races and tribes, that ye may show mutual recognition; verily, the most noble of you in Allah's eyes is the most pious; verily Allah is knowing, well-informed". Here, following the address, we have an indication of the subject that has called for treatment, then comes a declaration regarding it, and finally the passage is closed by a sententious maxim. This form is found not only in passages with direct address, but in a multitude of others. They begin by stating their occasion; a question has been asked, the unbelievers have said or done something, something has happened, or some situation has arisen. The matter is dealt with shortly, in usually not more than three or four verses; at the end comes a general statement, often about Allah, which rounds off the passage. Once we have caught this lilt of Qur'ān style it becomes fairly easy to separate the surahs into the separate pieces of which they have been built up, and this is a great step towards the interpretation of the Qur'ān. It is not, of course, to be too readily assumed that there is no connection between these separate pieces. There may, or there may not, be a connection in subject and thought, and where that is absent there may still be a connection in time. On the other hand, there may be no connection in thought between contiguous pieces, or the surah may have been built up of pieces of different dates that have been fitted into a sort of scheme.

Style of the Qur'ān.—It is only when we have unravelled these short units of composition which enter into the structure of the surahs that we can speak of the style of the Qur'ān. The insistence so frequently met with on its disjointedness, its formlessness, its excited, unpremeditated, rhapsodical character, rests too much on a failure to discern the natural divisions into which the surahs fall, and also to take account of the displacements and undesigned breaks in connection, which, as we shall see, are numerous. We have to remember, too, that Muhammad disclaimed being a poet, and evidently had no ear for poetry.[1] He claimed that he had messages to convey. We have to seek, therefore, for didactic, rather than for poetic or artistic, forms.

Slogans.—One of these forms, the prevailing one in later surahs, has been spoken of above. But the simplest form of the kind is the short statement introduced by the word "Say" There are about 250 of these scattered throughout the Qur'ān. Sometimes they stand singly; here and there we find groups of them standing together, though really quite distinct from each other, for instance in VI, 56 ff.; sometimes they are worked into the context of a passage. These statements are of various kinds, answers to questions, retorts to arguments or jeers of his opponents, statements of Muhammad's own position; there are one or two prayers, for example III, 25; there are two credal statements for his followers to repeat, the word "Say" being in the plural, II, 130, XXIX, 45, to which may be added CXII, though the verb is singular; finally, there are a number of phrases suitable for repetition in various circumstances, such as, "Allah's guidance is the guidance", II, 114, "Allah is my portion; on Him let the trusting set their trust", XXXIX, 39.

[1] See the story in Ibn Hishām, p. 882.

It is evident that these phrases were designed for repetition; they were not composed originally as parts of surahs, they were of the nature of slogans devised for public use, and found their way into surahs later. Where a context is given, usually in the later parts of the Qur'ān, we get a hint of how they were produced. A question has been asked, II, 185, 211, V, 6, VIII, 1, etc., or some argument or jeer has come to the Prophet's knowledge, and he has thought over it until the 'suggestion' of the answer has come. He has 'sought guidance' and has been told what to say. The statement thus becomes a part of one of the paragraphs already described as characteristic of Qur'ān style.

These slogans are difficult to date, and it is doubtful if any of those which appear in the Qur'ān are very early, though some of them may quite well be so. But they are so common that the presumption is that they were a constant element in Muhammad's methods of propaganda, and that from the first he made use of carefully prepared formulae for repetition.

The use of assonance in such formulae would be natural. But those which actually occur hardly support the idea that it was by this route that assonance became a feature of Muhammad's deliverances. Most of them fall naturally enough into the rhyme of the surah in which they occur, but few of them rhyme within themselves. XXXIV, 45 and XLI, 44 possibly do, and CII, 1, 2 looks like an early rhymed slogan, though not preceded by "Say". It is more likely that the suggestion of rhyme came from the *saj'* of the soothsayers.

Kāhin - Form.—Muhammad protested against being classed as a soothsayer, LII, 29, LXIX, 42, and, as the form and content of his deliverances developed, the disclaimer was justified; but to begin with, his position was similar enough to that of a *kāhin* to suggest that he may have taken a hint from the soothsayers as to the form of his utterances. Actually, there are five passages in the Qur'ān which are quite in *kāhin*-manner, XXXVII, 1-4, (5), LI, 1-6, LXXVII, 1-7, LXXIX, 1-14, C, 1-6. In these we have a number of oaths by females of some kind, forming a jingle, leading up to a statement which does not rhyme with the oaths. The statement is mostly quite short; but in LXXIX it is of some length and may have been extended. The feminine participles are usually thought to apply to angels; the Qur'ān itself gives some support to this, XXXVII, 165. But this is probably an afterthought, and it may be doubted if originally any definite meaning was attached to these asseverations. The soothsayers, no doubt, often used a string of cryptic oaths without much sense, simply to prepare the way for the statement and make it impressive.

Asseverative Passages.—Muhammad apparently found these random oaths unsatisfactory. LXXXIX, 1-4, which is so cryptic as to be unintelligible, may indicate this. LII, 1-8 still shows the same device of making the statement stand out by having a different assonance from the oaths, but the oaths, though still difficult to interpret, had evidently a clear enough sense in the Prophet's own mind. In other asseverative passages, of which there are not a few,[1] the oaths are chosen as having some bearing on the statement to which they lead up, and this statement in the same assonance makes an effective close to the passage. The best example is perhaps XCI, 1-10, where four pairs of oaths by contrasted things, sun and moon, day and night, heaven and earth, and what formed the soul and implanted in it its wickedness and piety, lead up to the statement of the contrast between him who purifies his soul and him who corrupts it. This asseverative style seems to have gradually been discarded. There are a number of passages where a single oath appears at the beginning, but in passages certainly Medinan oaths hardly appear at all.

'*When*'-*Passages.*—A modification of the asseverative passage is seen in the use of a number of temporal clauses, introduced by *idhā* or *yawma*, leading up to a statement pressing home the fact of the Judgment upon the conscience.

[1] A list of the chief asseverative passages may here be given: XXXVI, 1 ff., XXXVII, 1-4, XXXVIII, 1, XLIII, 1, XLIV, 1 ff., L, 1 ff., LI, 1-6, LII, 1-8, LIII, 1 ff., LVI, 74 ff., LXVIII, 1 ff., LXIX, 38-43, LXXIV, 35-40, LXXV, 1-6, LXXVII, 1-7, LXXIX, 1-14, LXXXI, 15-19, 22, 24, 25, 27, LXXXIV, 16-19, LXXXV, 1-7, LXXXVI, 1, 4, 11-14, LXXXIX, 1-4, XC, 1-4 ff., XCI, 1-10, XCII, 1-4 ff., XCIII, 1-3 ff., XCV, 1-5, C, 1-6, CIII, 1 f.

In one passage, LXXV, 26-30, it is a death-scene which is described in the temporal clauses, but usually it is the Last Day which is conjured up by a selection from its awe-inspiring phenomena. In LXXXIV, 1-6 the statement of the main clause is left unrhymed, but in all the others it has the same rhyme as the clauses which lead up to it. The longest of these passages is LXXXI, 1-14, where twelve *idhā*-clauses lead up to the statement: "A soul will know what it has presented", that is, the deeds laid to its account. The effectiveness of such a form is even more evident in some of the shorter pieces, and there can be no doubt that they were carefully designed for repetition to impress the conscience of hearers.[1]

Dramatic Scenes.—This homiletic purpose is evident throughout the Qur'ān. The piling up of temporal clauses did not continue, but at all stages of the Qur'ān the scenes of the Judgment and the future life are evoked, not for any speculative purpose, but in order to impress the conscience and clinch an argument. With all the details which the Qur'ān gives of the future abodes of the blessed and the damned, we nowhere get a complete description. Where such a picture seems to have been attempted, as in LV, LXXVI and LXXXIII, the attempt appears to break down in confusion. On the other hand we get short well-polished pieces describing luscious attractions or lurid terrors. The same applies to the descriptions of the Judgment; Muhammad evidently is interested in these scenes not for their own sake but for their homiletic value. Only once or twice does he make any attempt to describe the theophany, and it is not sustained, XXXIX, 67 ff., LXXXIX, 23 f. Attention should, however, be called to the dramatic quality of many of these scenes, which is often unrecognised, but which is really very effective. Some of them are difficult to understand, because, being designed for oral recitation, they do not indicate by whom the various speeches are made; that was

[1] 'When'-passages, introduced by *idhā*: LVI, 1-9 (LXIX, 13-17), LXXIV, 8-10, LXXV, 7-12, 26-30, LXXVII, 8-13, LXXIX, 34-41, LXXXI, 1-14, LXXXII, 1-5, LXXXIV, 1-6, XCIX, 1-6 (CX, 1-3); introduced by *yawma*: LXX, 8-14, LXXVIII, 18-26, LXXX, 34-37 (CI, 3-6).

left to be made clear by gesture or change of voice as the passage was delivered. As examples may be cited, L, 19-25 and XXXVII, 48-59; in both of these passages we have to use our imagination to supply the accompanying action of the speeches, but are rewarded by little dramatic scenes which must have been very telling if delivered with dramatic action. This dramatic quality is, in fact, a pervading characteristic of Qur'ān style. Direct speech is apt to be 'interjected' at any point, and we have to imagine the personages spoken of in the narrative as expressing themselves in words. If, for instance, we look at the story of Moses in XX, we find that more space is occupied by the spoken words of the actors than by actual narrative. Even where narrative does predominate, the story is hardly ever told straightforwardly, but tends to fall into a series of short word-pictures, the story advancing incident by incident, and the intervening links being left to the imagination of the hearers.

Narratives and Parables.—In narratives, too, the homiletic element is apt to intrude. Thus in the story of Joseph in XII, we find every now and then an aside introduced to make clear the intention of Allah in what happened. This homiletic element is also apt to intrude unduly into Qur'ān *mathals* or parables. The best of these is the parable of the Blighted Garden in LXVIII; that of the Two Owners of Gardens is less clear and more didactic, XVIII, 31-42. Others are little more than expanded similes, XIV, 29 ff., XVI, 77 f., XVIII, 43 f., XXX, 27, XXXIX, 30. That of the Unbelieving Town, XXXVI, 12 ff., is difficult to classify; it is perhaps a simile expanded into a story.

Similes.—The Qur'ān contains a good number of similes. These occur in all contexts. In descriptions of the Last Day, when the heavens are rolled up like a scroll, XXI, 104, when the people are like moths blown about, and the mountains are like carded wool, CI, 3, 4, the similes are sometimes borrowed with the rest of the material, but the Prophet had at all stages of his career a gift of coining vivid and sometimes grimly humorous comparisons. Jews who have the Torah but do not profit by it are compared to an ass loaded with books, LXII, 5. Some who in the early days in Medinah made advances to Muhammad and then drew back are likened to those who have lit a fire which has then gone out and left them more bewildered in the darkness than ever, II, 16; cf. 18 f. Polytheists who imagine other gods besides Allah are like the spider weaving its own frail house, XXIX, 40. The works of unbelievers, from which they hope to benefit at the Judgment, are like ashes blown away by the wind, XIV, 21, or like a mirage which appears to be water, but, when one comes to it, turns out to be nothing, XXIV, 39. People who pray to gods other than Allah are like those who stretch out their hands to water, which, however, never reaches their mouth, XIII, 15; the prayer of unbelieving Quraish at the Ka'bah is only whistling and clapping of hands, VIII, 35. Lukewarm supporters, asked for their opinion and getting up to speak, no doubt hesitatingly, are compared to logs of wood propped up, LXIII, 4. For other comparisons, see II, 166, 263, 266, 267, III, 113, VII, 175, X, 25, XVIII, 43, LVII, 19, LXXIV, 51. Where the simile is complicated by an attempt at allegory, the result is not so happy, XXX, 27, XXXIX, 30.

Metaphors.—Metaphors are still more common. T. Sabbagh [1] has collected well over four hundred metaphorical uses of words. Many of these, however, were, no doubt, already so much a matter of course as to be no longer felt as metaphorical. It is not easy to say how far the Qur'ān added new metaphors to the language. The number of commercial terms transferred to the religious sphere is noteworthy.[2] It is, of course, only what might be expected from Muhammad's upbringing, and his taking up his mission in a commercial town, but it did help to stamp its legalistic character upon Islam. The deeds of men are recorded in a book; the Judgment is the reckoning; each person receives his account; the balance is set up, and men's deeds are weighed; each soul is held in pledge for the deeds committed; if a man's actions are approved, he receives his reward, or his hire; to support the Prophet's cause is to lend

[1] T. Sabbagh, *La Métaphore dans le Coran.*
[2] C. C. Torrey, *The Commercial-Theological Terms in the Koran.*

to Allah. From Bedouin life come the designation of the delights of Paradise as *nuzul*, 'reception-feast', and the application of the verb *ḍalla*, 'to go astray', to those who follow false gods. The application of bodily functions to spiritual matters is almost unavoidable; thus unbelievers are deaf, unable to hear, blind, unable to see; they cannot discern the truth; they have veils over their hearts, heaviness in their ears; they are in darknesses. The revelation is guidance and light, and the function of a messenger is to lead people out of the darknesses into the light. Doubtful supporters are said to have disease in their hearts; after their conduct at Uḥud they are dubbed *munāfiqīn*, 'jinkers', 'those who dodge back into their holes like mice'.

Borrowed Metaphors and Words.—Many of these metaphors can be paralleled in Jewish and Christian literature. It must not, however, be too readily assumed that that is proof of their having been borrowed. Some of them are so obvious that they may quite well have been employed independently. Borrowed words, on the other hand, generally show their foreign origin by some peculiarity. That the Qur'ān contains a number of words which are not native Arabic was, a little reluctantly, recognised by Moslem scholars, though, in their lack of knowledge of other languages, they often failed to elucidate their origin. Modern scholarship has devoted a good deal of attention to these words, and with wider knowledge of the languages and dialects prevailing in the Near East in pre-Islamic times has for the most part succeeded in tracing their source. Here again, however, we must be on our guard against assuming that every word of foreign origin used in the Qur'ān was by that use introduced into Arabic. Apart from proper names, Dr. Jeffery[1] has collected some 275 words which have been regarded as of foreign origin. The majority of these, however, can be shown to have been in use in Arabic in pre-Islamic times, and many of them had become regular Arabic words. Of only about 70 can we say that the use was new, or that they were used in new senses. Of these 70, half

[1] Arthur Jeffery, *The Foreign Vocabulary of the Qur'ān*.

come from Christian languages, many from Syriac and a few from Ethiopic; some 25 come from Hebrew or Jewish-Aramaic; the rest, of little religious importance for the most part, come from Persian, Greek or unknown sources. It must, however, be remembered that between Syriac and Jewish-Aramaic the decision is often difficult, and the exact provenance of some of these words is still in dispute.

Language.—That there occur unfamiliar words and words used in an unfamiliar sense is shown by the fact that explanations are sometimes added. But it is only natural to assume that the Qur'ān was delivered in the language of the people so far as possible, and that even these borrowed words were already known to Muhammad's followers from their intercourse with Jews and Christians. As a matter of fact, the language of the Qur'ān, so far as we can judge, is on the whole the classical Arabic language. We have seen that in assonance at the end of verses inflectional vowels were dropped and the feminine ending modified, as in colloquial speech. How far this was done in the middle of the verses, we have no means of knowing. For, as the Qur'ān is now pointed and recited, these vowels and terminations are strictly exhibited and pronounced. This may be due to later revision and assimilation to the classical poetry, as Vollers [1] argues, and many dialectical forms may have been removed in the process. A few irregular forms, which we may perhaps assume to be colloquial or dialectical, still remain, for example, *yazzakkā* for *yatazakkā* (LXXX, 3, 7) *yadhdhakkaru* for *yatadhakkaru* (II, 272, III, 5, LXXX, 4), *iddāraka* for *tadāraka* (VII, 36, XXVII, 68).

The style of the Qur'ān is held to be unique and inimitable. It certainly is characteristic and unmistakable, in spite of its variations from surah to surah and from section to section.[2] Its artistic, dramatic, pictorial, imaginative qualities have often been lost sight of in theological treatment of the *I'jāz*, 'the inimitability' of the Qur'ān, but they have always exercised a spell upon the Moslem worshipper.

[1] K. Vollers, *Volkssprache und Schriftsprache im alten Arabien.*

[2] For the use of these as evidence of date, see Ch. VI.

CHAPTER V

THE COMPILATION OF THE SURAHS

REVISIONS AND ALTERATIONS

WE have seen that the unit of composition in the Qur'ān is not the surah, but the short piece. The surahs, except the very short ones, have been constructed rather than composed. The question then arises, whether they were put together by Muhammad, or by those who collected the Qur'ān after his death. The tradition as to the collection of the Qur'ān seems to leave the latter possibility open, and there are even special traditions which ascribe the placing of certain passages to Zaid b. Thābit. On the whole, however, Tradition seems to take it for granted that the surahs were found much in their present form. The question is one which has really never been thoroughly discussed, and which we shall probably never be able to answer with complete certainty. There is, however, a great deal of evidence that the Prophet himself had more to do with the compiling of the surahs than has been usually assumed. Some general considerations already mentioned argue against the collectors having had a free hand in the matter. The great variation in the lengths of the surahs is hardly to be accounted for by difference of subject or rhyme or form, though that may explain why some of the short pieces were kept as separate surahs. The occurrence of the *bismillah*, which we found reason to think belonged to the composition, would mark at least the beginning of a surah. The occurrence of the mysterious letters also seemed to imply that not only surahs, but also groups of surahs, were already in existence when the Qur'ān came to be arranged in its present order. The existence of surahs is borne out too by the challenge which the Prophet gave to his opponents that, if they believed that he had invented the Qur'ān, they should produce ten surahs like it, XI, 16. He must, at that time, have had at least ten pieces of the nature of surahs which he could produce if the challenge were taken up. The date is indeterminate, but is probably not later than early-Medinan times, and many other surahs may have taken shape within the Prophet's subsequent life-time. But the most conclusive proof of the Prophet's part in the compiling of the surahs comes from a detailed study of their structure, which discloses evidences of revisions and alterations such as could hardly have been made without his authority, and for which we can, in many cases, assign a reason in his own changing circumstances and aims.

That passages were not only placed in certain surahs, but were sometimes adapted to their position in them, is shown by the occurrence of hidden rhymes. The real explanation of what led Geyer to the assumption of a kind of sonnet-formation, is that passages which had originally rhymed in one assonance have been adapted to stand in a surah, the assonance of which is different. For example, XXIII, 12-16 rhyme in *-ī(l)*, the assonance of the surah as a whole; v. 14, however, is long, and breaks up into five short verses rhyming in *-ah*, with a rhyme-phrase added carrying the *-ī(l)* assonance, but not entering into the structure of the verse. The rhyme *-ah* can be found also in vv. 12 and 13 by dropping the end words of each, and this can be done with advantage to the sense. Thus we get in vv. 12-14 a complete little piece rhyming in *-ah* describing the generation of man as a sign of Allah's creative power. This has been fitted into the surah by adding rhyme-phrases and vv. 15, 16, which speak of the resurrection. The passage which follows, XXIII, 17-22, has been similarly dealt with. The rhyme-phrases are detachable, and, when they have been removed, traces of an assonance in *fāʿil* can be found underneath. Quite a number of other passages have been treated in this way.[1]

Attention may be called to a few cases in which the rhyme of the surah changes. The beginning of III rhymes in *-ā(l)*, as does also the end; the middle, however, has the

[1] See III, 30 ff., 40 ff., VII, 160 ff., X, 7-11, XIII, 2 ff., XIV, 29 ff., XVI, 10 ff., 50 f., 53., XXV, 47 ff., 55 ff., 62 f., XXVII, 60 ff., XXXII, 15-20, XL, 59 ff., 71 ff., XLI, 8 ff., XLIII, 8 ff.

rhyme in -*ī*(*l*). Near the point at which the change occurs stands a passage, v. 30 ff., dealing with the story of Mary and Jesus, which has originally rhymed in -*ā*(*l*) but into which phrases have been inserted to carry the rhyme, -*ī*(*l*). It is as if a portion with the latter rhyme had been inserted into a surah which had originally rhymed in -*ā*(*l*), and an attempt had been made to dovetail the two pieces together at the start. The impression is strengthened if we notice that the rhyme -*ī*(*l*) occurs at the end of v. 16, carried by a phrase the construction of which causes some difficulty and which leads over to v. 20 f. rather than to v. 17 f. In XIV also the rhyme changes in the middle of the surah and at the junction there is a passage, v. 29 ff., in which the original rhyme has been altered. In XIII something similar appears to have happened at the beginning, vv. 2-4, and in XIX near the middle, vv. 52-58, 59, but these cases are not quite so clear.

There are many passages in which the rhyme-phrases can be detached without revealing an older rhyme underneath. In these cases it is not quite so certain that revision has taken place, for, as we have seen, the detachable rhyme-phrase often appears as the mark of the close of a passage. When, however, it appears at the end of a number of consecutive verses, as in VI, 95 ff., it is reasonable to assume that it has been inserted into an originally unrhymed passage in order to give it the rhyme of the surah. In two cases this seems to have been done with a list of names, VI, 84 ff. and XXXVIII, 45 ff.; cf. also XIX, 52-58.

Nor is this the only way in which passages have been adapted. VI, 142-145 cannot be grammatically construed as they stand, but by taking the first part of each verse we get a list of Allah's bounties in produce of the soil and animals; into this, sentences have been introduced combating heathen food-taboos. In VII, 55 f. the sign of Allah's revival of dead land and the varying response of different soils—perhaps a simile of the varying response of men to the divine message—has been transformed by inserted sentences, marked by a sudden change of pronoun, into a corroboration of the resurrection.

If passages could be adapted to their place in a surah,

they could also be adapted to the needs of a different situation. The Qur'ān itself practically tells us that such revisions were made, for we are told that Satan may influence a prophet's formulation of his message, but Allah adjusts His signs and abrogates what Satan has thrown in, XXII, 51 ff. And the Prophet is assured that if he is made to forget a verse, he will be given a similar or a better one, II, 100. Moslem theology, too, founding on these and other passages, has always recognised that a deliverance may be modified or completely annulled by a subsequent one.[1] This is usually regarded as applying to separate deliverances, but XXII, 51 ff. seems to imply that alterations were made upon actual passages, and examination of the Qur'ān shows that both methods of revision were freely used.

Now, it is no doubt possible to revise a passage so carefully that no sign of patching remains, but as a rule a critical reader will detect the modification from some unevenness in the style. As a matter of fact, there are many such roughnesses in the Qur'ān. There are not only hidden rhymes and rhyme-phrases not woven into the texture of the passage, but there are abrupt changes of rhyme, and repetition of the same rhyme-word or -phrase in adjoining verses. Abrupt changes of subject are natural to the paragraph-style of the Qur'ān, but often we find a quite extraneous subject intruding into a passage apparently meant to be homogeneous. Or the same subject will be treated in somewhat different ways in neighbouring verses, often with repetition of words and phrases. There are breaks in grammatical construction which trouble the commentators. There are abrupt changes in the length of verses, and sudden changes of dramatic situation involving changes of pronoun from singular to plural, or from second to third person and vice versa. Sometimes apparently contradictory statements appear side by side. Passages of different dates stand together, and late phrases enter into earlier verses. So common are these things in the Qur'ān that they have often been regarded as characteristic of its style not calling for further study, but they certainly demand an explanation. The explanation may, of course,

[1] See note on the Moslem doctrine of Abrogation (pp. 98-99).

vary in each case, but in the great majority of cases it will be found in some revision or alteration of an earlier text.

Glosses, that is to say short explanations occasioned by some obscurity, which may be supposed to have been written on a manuscript by some later reader, are not numerous in the Qur'ān. Examples may be found in VI, 12, 20, VII, 90, XXI, 48, 104, XXVII, 7, XLI, 16, LXXVI, 16. How these have originated it is impossible to say, but in II, 79 we find one which is evidently considerably later than the writing of the original passage. Here the word *ikhrājuhum* is inserted to explain the pronoun *huwa*, but immediately in front of that is a phrase which evidently belongs to the preceding verse; when that is removed to its proper position, there is no difficulty about the reference of the pronoun; the insertion of *ikhrājuhum* must, therefore, be subsequent to the misplacement of the preceding phrase.

Explanations are sometimes added [1] in the form of an extension of the passage. In twelve places [2] we find after a rather unusual word or phrase the question: "What has let thee know what . . . is?" and this is followed by a short description. That in some the description has been added later is clear from the fact that it does not correspond to the sense in which the word or phrase was originally used. The most striking case is CI, 7 ff., but XC, 12 ff. and CIV, 5 ff. are similar, and the addition is never an exact definition.

There are additions and insertions of other kinds, of which the following are examples taken from the shorter surahs. In XCI it is evident that the passage, when composed, ended at v. 10 (see above, p. 76), but this is followed by a summary of the story of Thamūd, which may have been added to illustrate the moral, or placed here just because of the similar rhyme. LXXXVIII, 6, 7 are marked as an insertion by the different rhyme, LXXVIII, 33, 34, by breaking the connection between 32 and 35. In LXXXVII a sudden change in the dramatic situation at v. 16 marks an addition which might possibly be contemporary—as if the Prophet, having recited

[1] See p. 81.

[2] LXIX, 3, LXXIV, 27, LXXVII, 14, LXXXII, 17, LXXXIII, 8, 9, LXXXVI, 2. XC, 12, XCVII, 2, CI, 2, 7, CIV, 5.

his revelation, had turned to impress its point upon his audience—but is probably much later. In LXXIV, vv. 31-34 are clearly marked as an insertion by the different style and length of verse. Some of these examples already suggest that Muhammad himself was responsible for the addition, though it is possible to hold that they were due to some later collector or reader.

There are, however, other additions which can hardly have been made without authority. The misplaced phrase of II, 79, for instance, though it looks like a gloss written on the margin and taken in by a copyist at the wrong place, makes a real addition to the regulation laid down. There are not many such misplacements, but short additions which make substantial alterations to the sense are frequent enough. In LXXIV, 55 we have a limitation of the freedom of man's choice which virtually takes back what had been stated in 54; cf. LXXVI, 30 f., LXXXI, 29. This corresponds to the hardening of the doctrine of predestination which took place in Medinan days. Reservations introduced by *illā*, ' except ', are specially frequent. We must not, of course, assume that every such reservation is a later addition, but in quite a number of cases [1] there are independent reasons for such an assumption, as in LXXXVII, 7, and XCV, 6, where *illā* introduces a longer verse with characteristic Medinan phraseology into an early passage with short rhythmic verses. Such additions, making as they do a distinct modification of the statement, must have been deliberately introduced. In at least some of them we can discern the motive for making the exception.

Longer additions can sometimes be easily distinguished. Thus in LXXIII a long verse occurs at the end which, by containing a reference to Moslems being engaged in fighting, is clearly marked as Medinan, and is recognised by everyone as being so. But the rest of the surah, and especially the beginning, is in the short crisp verses characteristic of early passages. The reason for the addition is that the passage at

[1] II, 155, 229, 282, III, 83, IV, 145, XI, 14, XIX, 61, 90, XXIII, 6 f., XXV, 70, XXVI, 227, LIII, 27, LXXVIII, 25, LXXXIV, 25, LXXXVII, 7, LXXXVIII, 23 f., XCV, 6, CIII, 3.

the beginning, which really refers to the composition of the Qur'ān,[1] had been adapted so as to recommend night-prayer; but as this was being overdone, it became necessary in Medinah to counsel moderation.

Additions in the middle of surahs are very common. A few examples will suffice. The first part of XIX has the assonance in *-īyā*, but this is interrupted by vv. 35-41, which have the common *-ī(l)* assonance. These verses follow an account of Mary and Jesus, and, by rejecting the idea of Allah having offspring, were evidently meant to combat the Christian doctrine of the Son of God. III, 125-128 warn against the taking of excessive interest, and promise heavenly reward to those who act generously. The passage evidently closed with the rhyme-phrase of v. 128, but two verses follow giving a further description of those who do well by repenting and asking forgiveness, and a promise of heavenly reward which is practically a repetition of that already made. Those who have transgressed but are prepared to reform are thus included. XXII, 5-8 argue for the resurrection as in line with Allah's power otherwise manifest, and close with a scoff at those who "without knowledge, guidance, or light-giving book" argue to the contrary. Verses 9, 10 join to this rather awkwardly and threaten not only future punishment, but "humiliation in this life", a Medinan threat, to those who so act. The change of tone and attitude shows clearly enough that these verses did not belong to the original passage. In XXXVII we have accounts of various Biblical persons, closing in the first four cases with the refrain; "Thus do We reward those who do well. Verily he is one of Our servants believing." But in the case of Abraham this refrain is followed by a statement about the posterity of Abraham and Isaac. This must have been added after the passage was composed.

Then we often find that a passage has alternative continuations, which follow each other in the present text. This will be marked by a break in sense, and by a break in grammatical construction, the connection being not with what immediately precedes, but with what stands some distance

[1] See Bell, *Origin of Islam in its Christian Environment*, p. 97 f.

back; there may also be the repetition of a word or phrase. Thus in XXIII we find following upon v. 65, which speaks of men continuing a defective course of conduct, three passages introduced by *ḥattā idhā*, 'until when', v. 66, v. 79 and v. 101. It is possible, with some straining, to join v. 79 to v. 78, but v. 101 will not join to v. 100. But *ḥattā idhā* requires before it a reference to something continuing. Verses 101 f. are in fact the proper continuation of v. 65, as is evident if we read them together; the other verses introduced by *ḥattā idhā* are substituted for them. In V, v. 46 begins with a phrase *sammāʿūna li-l-kadhib*, which is entirely out of connection. The same phrase occurs in v. 45, and we can quite well replace it and what follows of v. 45 by v. 46. At the end of XXXIX there is a verse which appears isolated. It follows a Judgment-scene and evidently belongs to it; but the scene is already finished; judgment has been given, the unbelievers have been sent to Gehennah, the pious have entered the Garden; then we find ourselves back at the scene of Judgment where judgment will be given with truth. This phrase, which has already occurred in v. 69, indicates what was the original position of v. 75; it followed the first phrase of v. 69 and completed the scene; at some later stage it was displaced by the much longer description in vv. 69-74.[1] Occasionally a change of rhyme may accompany such a substitution, as in LXXX, where vv. 34-37 have their assonance in *-īh*, while vv. 38-42, which join equally well to v. 33, have the *-ah* assonance which runs through the whole of the rest of the surah. More frequently the occurrence of the same rhyme-word or -phrase is a sign that such a substitution has been made, the new version being made to end with the same rhyme as that which it replaced. Thus in II, vv. 96 and 97 both end in *law kānū yaʿlamūna*, which gives a presumption that v. 97 was intended to replace v. 96; in III, the similar

[1] To give a full list of such substitutes is tedious and unnecessary. Some of the more striking cases may be here listed: II, 95 ff., 129 ff., 139 ff., 179 ff., 192 ff., III, 43 f., 61 ff., 97 ff., 106 ff., 137 ff., 145 f., 164 f., 177 ff., IV, 27 ff., 130 f., V, 45 f., 52 ff., 76 ff., 92 f., VI, 87 ff., VII, 38 f., 163 ff., VIII, 73 f., IX, 87 ff. (82 ff.), 112 f., 118 f., X, 104 ff., XI, 42 ff., XIII, 19 ff., XV, 87 ff., XVI, 16 ff., XVII, 47, XXVII, 38 ff., XXXIV, 50 ff., XXXV, 26 ff., XXXVI, 79 ff., XXXIX, 48 f., 69 ff., XL, 31 ff., XLV, 26 ff., L, 21 ff., LIV, 43 ff., LVII, 13 f., LIX, 5 ff., LXIII, 7 f., LXXII, 26 ff., LXXIV, 31 ff., LXXX, 33 ff.

ending indicates that v. 138 is a substitute for v. 139. See also IX, 118 and 119, XXXIV, 51 and 52, XLV, 27 and 28, LXXII, 25 and 26-28. It may be noted that in such cases the alternative continuations often stand in reverse order of date, though one cannot take this as an invariable rule. It is as if the paper [1] had been cut and the alternative inserted. Occasionally we may find a substitution made at the beginning or in the middle of a passage, as if an alternative had been written above or between the lines, or two versions may be interwoven, as in III, 122-124, as if the substitution had been somehow written through a text already written down; cf. XXXVI, 1-4.

The conviction that we have here written documents grows upon us as we deal with these evidences of revision, and an assumption that such is the case seems necessary to explain another phenomenon of frequent occurrence in the Qur'ān. There remains a multitude of disconnected pieces, sudden changes of subject, even grammatical breaks, which no discursiveness of style or additions or alternative continuations will explain. Take, for instance, LXXXIV, 16-19; here we have a little piece in *kāhin*-style, a number of cryptic oaths, followed by an emphatic statement. It is evidently complete in itself, has its own rhyme, and has no apparent connection in thought with the rest of the surah. How did it come to stand where it does? A collector may have thrown it in at random, but a responsible collector would, one might think, have sought a more suitable place. The same thing appears in LXXV, 16-19 and LXXXVIII, 17-20. In these two cases it is fairly evident that immediately before the unconnected piece an addition has been made to the preceding passage, for the added verses have a different rhyme. In LXXXIV there is no abrupt change of rhyme, but if we consider carefully we shall see that vv. 13-15 destroy the balance of the preceding piece, vv. 7-12, which is complete as it stands, two verses being given to describing the fate of each class. In each case, then, an addition has been made, and the addition occupies approximately the same space as the

[1] "Paper" is used in the general sense of writing material of whatever nature that may have been. Papyrus sheets seem probable.

extraneous passage which follows. The presence of this latter would be explained if we were to suppose that it had stood on the back of a scrap of paper on which the addition was written, and that both sides of the paper had been read and copied consecutively when the Qur'ān came to be made up in the form of a codex. Similar examples may be found throughout the Qur'ān. To take an example from near the beginning: II, 16 compares those who have accepted the Prophet's guidance and then gone back upon it to people who have lit a fire, and then it has gone out, leaving them blinded in the darkness. Verse 17, "Deaf, dumb and blind, they do not return", evidently closes the passage, but vv. 18, 19 contain another simile: they are like people in a thunder-storm, the rain pours down, the thunder deafens them, the lightning blinds them. Evidently this is a parallel to v. 16 and should have preceded v. 17. It has been added later. There follows a passage, vv. 19b, 20, quite unconnected with the context, appealing for the worship of Allah and adducing signs of His power and bounty. This appears to be continued, after a break, in vv. 26, 27. Now v. 25, while not evidently an addition, is probably so, for v. 24 finishes with a reference to the "reprobate", which is conclusive enough. But v. 25 proceeds to describe a special class of "reprobates", who violate a covenant after having made it. Further, we find in vv. 158-160a a passage which, by the use of the rather unusual word *andād*, 'peers', is marked as almost certainly a continuation of vv. 19b, 20, 26, 27. Here we have, not preceding but following, a passage, vv. 160b-162, which returns to the theme of vv. 156, 157, and must have been intended as an addition to that passage. This whole section is an interesting example of how a passage has been expanded by additions. The point, however, here is that we find a passage originally dealing with the worship of Allah apparently cut up, and the back of the pieces used for making insertions into other passages.

An interesting example of the same kind is found in surah IX. The last two verses of this surah are said by Tradition to have come to the knowledge of Zaid b. Thābit when he had almost completed his task of collecting the

Qur'ān, and were placed here as the most convenient position at the time. This is evidently an attempt to account for the fact that there is a break in connection between v. 128 and v. 129, and between v. 129 and v. 130. These two verses seem to stand isolated, but v. 130 will connect well enough with v. 128, though the latter verse ends as if nothing more were to be said. It is a case of something having been later added to a passage, and we may suppose that the back of v. 129 was used to write it on. By some accident (v. 128 had itself been used for the writing of another passage) the back was read by the compilers before the addition. But this is not all; v. 40 of the same surah stands isolated, though it evidently requires something in front of it. The pronoun "him" must evidently refer to the Prophet, of whom there has been no mention in the context, but v. 129 speaks of the Prophet, and if we read v. 129 and v. 40 together we get a moving appeal for loyalty to the Prophet addressed to his followers. This has evidently been cut in two, one part being added to v. 128 and the other placed after v. 39.

The reverse seems also to have taken place; scraps of paper were somehow pasted together to form a sheet. XIV, 8-17—an evident addition to the account of Moses—in which he addresses his people in regular Qur'ān style, is followed by a series of disjointed pieces, vv. 18-20, 21, 22, 24-27, 28, which together occupy practically the same space. In fact, it is almost a rule in the later parts of the Qur'ān that an addition or connected deliverance of any length is preceded or followed by a number of disconnected pieces which together make up approximately the same length. An interesting instance of this occurs at the end of II. There we find a long deliverance dealing with the recording of debts, vv. 282, 283. This occupies approximately the same space as vv. 278-281, a deliverance forbidding usury, v. 284 a separate verse, and vv. 285, 286 a profession of faith of the believers. Into this piece two little sentences intrude at the junction of the verses; they have no connection with each other or with the context and break the connection of v. 285 and v. 286, which must have originally formed one verse. If now we suppose the deliverance regarding debts, v. 282 f., to have been written on the back of a sheet (or part of a sheet) which contained the deliverance on usury, vv. 278-281, and on that of a second sheet containing vv. 284, 285 f., we find that the intrusion into the latter piece comes practically opposite a proviso introduced into the debts-deliverance excepting from its scope transactions in the market where goods pass from hand to hand. This we may suppose was written on the back of two scraps and inserted into the deliverance. To do so, the sheet was cut and the proviso pasted in. Hence the appearance of two extraneous scraps on the other side of the sheet.

The same thing occurs in IV, where, if we suppose vv. 90-93 to have been written on the back of vv. 81-89, a proviso introduced by *illā*, v. 92a, will come opposite v. 84 which breaks the connection between v. 83 and v. 85. This passage is further interesting in that the passage vv. 81-83, 85, 86 is almost certainly private and was not meant to be publicly recited. There are quite a number of passages of this kind included in the Qur'ān. The most striking of them is III, 153, which can hardly have been intended for publication either at the time or later; cf. also vv. 148c and 155.

As further proof that these alterations and revisions belong to Muhammad's life-time, we may consider some of the passages dealing with subjects and situations which we know to have presented critical problems to him. It is just at these points that the Qur'ān becomes most confused.

A simple case is that of the ord inance concerning fasting. When he removed to Medinah, Muhammad hoped for support from the Jews and showed himself willing to learn from them. Tradition says that he introduced the Jewish fast of the *'Āshūrā*, which was the Day of Atonement, preceded by some days of special devotion. Later, the month of Ramaḍān was prescribed. Now, in II, 179-181 these two things lie side by side: v. 180 prescribes a fast of a certain number of days, v. 181 the month of Ramaḍān. The two verses are, of course, generally read consecutively, the certain number of days of v. 180 being regarded as made more precise by the mention of the month of Ramaḍān in v. 181.

But a certain number of days is not naturally equivalent to a month, and the repetition of phrases in the two verses shows that the one was intended to replace the other. We have, in fact, a case of alternative continuations of v. 179. Further, we find that v. 182 is entirely unconnected; not only has it no reference to fasting, but whereas in the preceding verses the believers are being addressed and Allah spoken of in the third person, in it Allah is speaking, the Prophet is being addressed, and men spoken of in the third person. Verse 183 returns to the subject of fasting and the dramatic setting of vv. 179-182. If we consider the length of v. 181, we shall find that when written out it occupies approximately the same space as v. 180 and v. 182 together. The presence of this latter verse seems to have arisen from the necessity of adding to the space afforded by the back of v. 180 by using the back of a verse from some other context.

The marriage laws in surah IV are a clear case of alternative continuations. Verse 27 lays down the forbidden degrees of relationship, and reproduces the Mosaic list with some adaptation to Arab custom. That this was deliberate is shown by v. 31, which states that " Allah desireth . . to guide you in the customs of those who were before you ". At a later time, however, some relaxation appeared necessary, and vv. 29, 30 and perhaps 32a were substituted for v. 31, allowing marriage with slaves. Finally v. 28, which gives ample liberty, was substituted for vv. 29, 30, and v. 32b was added to give a verse-ending. The similar endings of vv. 31, 32a and 32b show that substitutions have been made.

The change of *qiblah* affords another example. The passage dealing with it, II, 136-147, is very confused; vv. 139-147 especially are unintelligible as they stand. When analysed, however, they turn out to contain (*a*) a private revelation to the Prophet of the solution to his problem, vv. 139a, 144; (*b*) a public announcement, using part of (*a*) accompanied by an appeal for obedience based on gratitude, vv. 139a, 145-147; and (*c*) the final form of the ordinance, vv. 139a, 139b.

The process of the introduction of the religion of Abraham is outlined for us in II, 124-135 It takes the form of answers to the assertion of Jews and Christians: v. 129a, "They say: 'Be ye Jews or Christians and ye will be guided'". This is followed by three retorts introduced by "Say". Verses 133-135 claim that the Prophet and his followers have a perfect right to serve Allah in their own way, as did Abraham and the patriarchs who were an independent religious community long since passed away. This passage was cut off and replaced by vv. 130, 132, in which it is claimed that Muhammad and his followers stand in the line of Abraham and the patriarchs, Moses, Jesus and all the prophets. It was again modified by the insertion of v. 131 in place of v. 132. Finally, the short retort of v. 129b was written in, professing the creed of Abraham, who was a *ḥanīf* and no polytheist. The back of the discarded passages was then utilised to add an account of the transmission of the religion of Abraham to his sons. This now stands as vv. 124-128, having been put before v. 129, and not after it as was evidently intended.

The question of the pilgrimage, which was part of the religion of Abraham, also caused difficulty. The ceremony was recognised and Muhammad's followers were counselled to take part in it, but as *ḥanīfs*, followers of the religion of Abraham, not as polytheists, XXII, 32. Sacrificial animals were to be sent to Meccah, vv. 35a, 34. But the bloodshed to which Moslem attacks on Meccan caravans, and especially the clash at Badr, led, made it dangerous for any Moslem to visit Meccah. It was therefore laid down that the animals dedicated for sacrifice might be slaughtered at home and their flesh given to the poor. This we can deduce from XXII, 30-38.[1]

Fighting in the sacred months also caused difficulty. Muhammad's attitude is made clear by the analysis of surah IX. They were at first recognised as a period of truce, by a deliverance which consisted of IX, 36a, 2, 5, but as the intercalary month, which kept the Arab lunar year in conformity with the seasons, was decreed from Meccah, misunderstandings as to what months were sacred would soon arise. Hence the deliverance which now stands as IX, 36,

[1] See my article 'The Origin of the *'īd al-aḍḥā*', *The Moslem World*, XXIII (1933), p. 117 ff.

37, abolishing the intercalary month and decreeing that war with the polytheists was to be carried on continuously.

The discarded verses dealing with the sacred months now appear as vv. 2 and 5, because the back of them was used, with other material, for the writing of a renunciation of agreements with polytheists, in fact the denunciation of the treaty of Ḥudaibiyah which stands at the beginning of IX. As the heading informs us, however, this is also a proclamation to be made at the pilgrimage. It has been altered and added to for this purpose after the fall of Meccah.[1]

The defeat of the Moslems at Uḥud was naturally a severe blow to the prestige of the Prophet. The passage dealing with the battle, III, 97 ff., is in great confusion. Analysis shows that there was an address intended for delivery before the battle, which consisted of vv. 97, 98, 99, 106a, 111-113, 119, 133-137, 139-144, 152, 154. Part of this, perhaps from v. 133 onward, was redelivered, with a few alterations, some time after the battle. Reactions to the defeat appear in a reproof to the Prophet himself for having, without authority, promised the assistance of angels, vv. 117, 120, 121 and parts of vv. 122-124. That was later revised as an explanation and rebuke to his followers. That he had been inclined to speak angrily to them is indicated in the private verse, 153. Part of this "rough" speech may be embedded in vv. 145-148, a passage which has been revised and added to in a milder sense later. In fact, we can see the attitude to the defeat growing gradually calmer and more kindly towards the faithful. Finally, when the set-back had been overcome, part of the original address was used again, with a new continuation added after v. 106a, in preparation probably for the attack on the Jewish tribe of Naḍīr, vv. 106b-110; and the back of a discarded piece was used for the writing of an ordinance prohibiting usury, which has thus come to be mixed up with the Uḥud material.[2]

Treated in this way the Qur'ān certainly becomes much

[1] See my article 'Muhammad's Pilgrimage Proclamation', *J.R.A.S.* (1937), p. 233 ff.

[2] For my analysis of other complicated passages, see *The Moslem World*, XXII (1932) 'The Men on the A'rāf' (VII, 44); XXXVIII (1948) 'Sūrat al Ḥashr (LIX).

more intelligible. Much remains obscure, not only because the analysis is uncertain, but because we do not know enough of the circumstances. But we can at least discern something of the way in which Muhammad inspired and guided the nascent community of Islam. Occasionally we even get a glimpse into the inner mind of the Prophet, and learn something of his plans, his occasional misgivings and self-reproaches, and his ever-renewed assurance.

It seems clear, then, that the present form of the Qur'ān, which is practically the form given to it at the revision in the reign of 'Othman, rests upon written documents which go back to Muhammad's life-time. Whether these were written by his own hand is really immaterial. We know that in his later years he employed secretaries, and there are even traditions which tell of them being employed in writing the revelation. It is, in fact, difficult to believe that no record was made of the legal deliverances, often of some length, which were given in Medinah. But if we read between the lines of LXXXVII, 1-9, we may gather that he distrusted his memory, and suspect that he very early took to writing out his *qur'āns* and memorising them beforehand. That he kept the fact secret is possible, though XXV, 6 implies that it was at least suspected in Meccah. Secrecy may help to explain the scarcity of writing material which led to backs of sheets and scraps being used, though perhaps the fact that Medinah was not a trading community like Meccah may be sufficient to explain it. That the 'Othmanic recension was based upon *ṣuḥuf*, or ' sheets ' which were found in the possession of Ḥafṣah, we know. Tradition asserts these to have been the collection of the Qur'ān made by Zaid b. Thābit after Muhammad's death. We have seen above (p. 39) that this tradition is open to various criticisms, and in particular it is difficult to see how such an official collection, if it was made, came to be in the possession of Ḥafṣah, even though she was the daughter of the caliph 'Omar. She was, however, also one of the widows of the Prophet, and as likely as any of his wives to have been entrusted with the care of precious documents. The *ṣuḥuf* may have been in her possession, not as 'Omar's daughter, but as Muhammad's widow.

NOTE ON THE MOSLEM DOCTRINE OF *NĀSIKH* AND *MANSŪKH*

This doctrine is based on verses of the Qur'ān:

II, 100: " For whatever verse We cancel or cause (the messenger) to forget, We bring a better or the like ".

XIII, 39: " Allah deleteth or confirmeth what He willeth; with Him is the mother of the Book ".

XVI, 103: " When We substitute one verse for another—Allah knoweth best what He sendeth down—they say: 'Thou art simply an inventor'; nay, most of them have not knowledge ".

XXII, 51: " We have not sent a messenger or prophet before thee, but when he formulated his desire Satan threw (something) into his formulation; so Allah abrogateth what Satan throweth in, then Allah adjusteth His signs "

What is referred to in the last verse is supposed to have been completely removed, so as not to occur in the Qur'ān.

The doctrine has been voluminously discussed in Islam, not from the point of view of literary criticism, but from that of Law, it being important for Islam to decide what ordinances of the Qur'ān were abrogated and what remained valid. In some respects the doctrine was extended, on the one hand to include the abrogation of laws of the Pagan Arabs, or of Jews or Christians, through the revelation of the Qur'ān, and on the other to admit the possibility of an ordinance of the Qur'ān being abrogated by the Sunnah. Ash-Shāfi'i, however, laid it down that when this happened there must be something in the Qur'ān to confirm the Sunnah. Others held that the proper sense of *naskh* was that one verse of the Qur'ān abrogated another, and that in regard to this we must not follow the opinions of exegetes or the founders of legal schools, but have the authority of a direct statement of the Prophet or of one of the Companions, though it might be possible to infer *naskh* from plain contradiction of two verses, combined with a knowledge of their dates. Other restrictions of the doctrine were introduced; it applies only to commands, not to narratives or promises or threats; alterations of practice, such as the recommendation of patience in Meccah and fighting in Medinah, are not properly included under abrogation, but are rather instances of postponement of promulgation of the full law of Islam because of unsuitable circumstances. There are other cases in which, though a different law is laid down, it remains allowable to act according to the earlier one. As-Suyūṭī in his *Itqān*, adopting these restrictions, reduces the number of cases of abrogation proper to twenty, of which he gives a list.

One should not perhaps expect the result of such legal discussion to confirm results of literary analysis, though in a few instances it does. What interests us is that Islam does recognise that deliverances were sometimes replaced by others. Further, the fact that these abrogated deliverances have been retained in the Qur'ān as it has come down to us, affords a strong presumption that no attempt was made to adapt it to any preconceived ideas. The retention of the recitation, with abrogation of the ordinance, is a difficulty for Islam. As-Suyūṭī gives two grounds, (*a*) the abrogated verses were the Word of Allah, which it was meritorious to recite; (*b*) abrogation was generally directed to making things easier, and the earlier ordinance was retained as a reminder of God's mercy.

CHAPTER VI

THE CHRONOLOGICAL ORDER OF THE QUR'ĀN

It would be a great step towards the understanding of the Qur'ān if we could arrange its contents in the order in which they were produced. To this problem much attention has naturally been devoted. The headings of the surahs already describe them as Meccan or as Medinan. But these statements do not carry us very far, even if we take them as reliable. For it has always been recognised that these indications of origin do not necessarily apply to all the contents of the surahs to which they are prefixed, and that surahs may contain passages of differing dates. Tradition has concerned itself largely with the historical occasion of individual passages, and has sought to find definite events and concrete personalities with which to associate them. But the principles already laid down as to the use of Tradition (p. 20) must apply here also. In many Medinan passages the reference to external events about which there is independent tradition is perfectly clear. But in the great bulk of the Qur'ān there is either no reference to historical events, or the events and circumstances to which reference is made are not otherwise known. In regard to such passages there are often differing traditions, and as often as not the stories related to explain them turn out, when critically examined, to be imagined from the passages themselves. This applies particularly to Meccan, or supposedly Meccan, passages, where in the absence of definite information imaginative exegesis had free play. In any case, in the dearth of fixed events in the Meccan period, the order of the Meccan surahs cannot be regarded as fixed by Tradition. There is, in effect, no reliable tradition as to the historical order of the Qur'ān. We are thrown back upon study of the book itself, and have to base any chronological arrangement upon internal evidence, except in so far as references to known events fix the dates of a number of passages.[1]

Several attempts to work out the chronological order of the surahs have been made by Western scholars. The one which has found most acceptance is that given by Noeldeke in his *Geschichte des Korans* (1860). It was based on critical use of Tradition, and on grounds of style, phraseology, and the manner of setting forth the doctrines stressed at different times. It assumes a sort of progressive deterioration of style beginning with exalted poetical passages, and gradually becoming more prosaic.

Noeldeke distinguishes, as Moslem scholars do, two great periods in the composition of the Qur'ān, the Meccan and the Medinan. But within the Meccan period he distinguishes three sub-periods into which the surahs are grouped. Those of the first are mostly quite short. The verses also are short and the language rhythmic and full of imagery. Groups of oaths often occur at the beginning of passages in this sub-period. The surahs belonging to it are XCVI, LXXIV, CXI, CVI, CVIII, CIV, CVII, CII, CV, XCII, XC, XCIV, XCIII, XCVII, LXXXVI, XCI, LXXX, LXVIII, LXXXVII, XCV, CIII, LXXXV, LXXIII, CI, XCIX, LXXXII, LXXXI, LIII, LXXXIV, C. LXXIX, LXXVII, LXXVIII, LXXXVIII, LXXXIX, LXXV, LXXXIII, LXIX, LI, LII, LVI, LXX, LV, CXII, CIX, CXIII, CXIV, I.

In the second sub-period, we see the transition from the sublime enthusiasm of the first to the greater calmness of the third. The Prophet seeks to explain his dogmas by numerous illustrations from nature and history. Discussions of dogmas begin to appear. In particular, the signs of Allah's power in nature and in the stories of former prophets are treated. To these latter a turn is given so that they have a bearing upon Muhammad's own experiences. New modes of speech are to be seen. The oaths of the first period are seldom used. The surahs grow longer, and frequently have formal introductions, such as: "This is the revelation of Allah . . .". Passages are often introduced by *qul* 'say'. The use of *ar-Raḥmān* as a proper name for God belongs to this period. The surahs belonging to it are: LIV, XXXVII, LXXI, LXXVI, XLIV, L, XX, XXVI, XV, XIX, XXXVIII, XXXVI, XLIII, LXXII, LXVII, XXIII, XXI, XXV, XVII, XXVII, XVIII.

In the third sub-period, the use of *ar-Raḥmān* as a proper name is dropped, but the other characteristics of the second are intensified.

[1] An arrangement based on Tradition is given in the surah-headings of the official Egyptian printed edition; see the table at the end of the chapter.

The prophetic stories are repeated almost to weariness. The surahs belonging to it are: XXXII, XLI, XLV, XVI, XXX, XI, XIV, XII, XL, XXVIII, XXXIX, XXIX, XXXI, XLII, X, XXXIV, XXXV, VII, XLVI, VI, XIII.

In the Medinan period there is not so much change of style as change of subject. The Prophet, being now head of a community, issues laws and commands in the name of Allah. Often the people are directly addressed, and historical events are dealt with in didactic fashion. The surahs of this period are: II, XCVIII, LXIV, LXII, VIII, XLVII, III, LXI, LVII, IV, LXV, LIX, XXXIII, LXIII, XXIV, LVIII, XXII, XLVIII, LXVI, LX, CX, XLIX, IX, V.

Sir William Muir in his *Life of Mahomet* gave an independent arrangement of the surahs. It differs from Noeldeke's mainly in placing a number of passages dealing with the wonders of nature earlier than Muhammad's Call to be a prophet. Rodwell in his *Translation of the Qur'ān* adopted Noeldeke's order with a few changes in the position of the surahs of the earliest group. Grimme in his *Muhammad* (Part II, p. 25 ff.) gave an arrangement which made more prominent to the doctrinal characteristics of the surahs. He distinguished two main groups of Meccan origin. The first proclaims monotheism, resurrection and judgment, and future life of bliss or torment; man is free to believe or not; Muhammad makes no claim to be a prophet, but is only a preacher. The second group introduces God's *raḥmah*, ' mercy ' or ' grace ', with which the name *ar-Raḥmān* is associated; the revelation of the Book becomes prominent, and stories of former recipients of revelation are recounted. Between these two groups come a number of intermediate surahs in which the Judgment is represented as near, and stories of punishment upon unbelieving peoples are told. H. Hirschfeld in his *New Researches into the Composition and Exegesis of the Qur'ān* made a radical departure from Noeldeke's scheme and founded his arrangement on the character of the passages as original revelation, confirmatory, declamatory, narrative, descriptive or legislative. The interest of this is that it recognises that it is passages rather than surahs with which we have to deal, but it has not found much acceptance. R. Blachère (*Le Coran*) returns to an arrangement based upon Noeldeke's, but he gives more weight to the development of Moslem worship and of direct opposition to polytheism. He also divides some of the surahs into portions of different dates, but this is vitiated by failure to discern the natural points of division.

As a first approximation to the historical order of the Qur'ān Noeldeke's arrangement is useful. But the criterion of style seems to play too large a part in it. That Muhammad's style did change, no reader of the Qur'ān will be disposed to deny. But we cannot assume that the change was due simply to the waning of his initial emotion and enthusiasm. Emotion may recur, and style may be deliberately adopted to suit varying ends in view. There are, in fact, passages in the Qur'ān which seem to suggest that different styles were used at the same time for different kinds of utterances, for instance, XLVII, 12. It is doubtful, too, if the use of *ar-Raḥmān* as a proper name can, as Noeldeke held, be limited to the middle-Meccan period. It may have been introduced then, but there is no record of its having been deliberately dropped, and the Meccans who objected to its use in the heading of the protocol of the treaty of Ḥudaibiyah evidently regarded it as a kind of proper name when used in the *bismillah*. Apart from such details, it is further to be noted that Noeldeke's scheme is a grouping of the surahs as unities. He did recognise that occasionally passages of different dates had found their way into the same surah, but on the whole he retained the surahs in their traditional form. Subsequent scholars, while still retaining the surah itself as the fundamental unit and showing reluctance to admit breaks in its composition, have tended to see more intrusion of later passages into early surahs. But if, as has been argued above, the unit of composition in the Qur'ān was the short passage, and the surahs were afterwards compiled from such pieces, the date of the separate passages becomes a prior question. There may be a slight presumption that passages of about the same date would be placed in the same surah, but it is at least possible that surahs may have originally been made up of passages composed at different times. And if both passages and surahs have been subjected to later revisions in Muhammad's own life-time, the problem becomes more complicated still. It may well be doubted, indeed, whether any complete arrangement of the Qur'ān in chronological order can be made. The best that can be done here is to lay down some general principles and outline a scheme into which the composition of the Qur'ān may be fitted.

Any attempt to arrange the Qur'ān in chronological order must be based on a careful analysis of the surahs. This, while complicating the problem, will often give us hints as to the relative priority of ideas and forms of expression. The attempt will have to be based on careful exegesis also. The traditional interpretation naturally reads back the developed system of Moslem theology into the Qur'ān wherever possible. But we have no right to read into any passage more than it actually says; we must endeavour to understand it in the sense which it had when first delivered.

In the absence of references to historical events, style is a useful criterion of relative date. For there is no doubt that the short crisp verse and studied rhyme belong to an earlier stage than the loose trailing verse and mechanical rhyme formed by grammatical terminations. But, as we have seen, this may be modified by other considerations, and is by no means decisive. Phraseology is perhaps a more reliable criterion. Certain turns of phrase belong to certain periods and developments of teaching and controversy. But here also there are cautions to be observed. A word or phrase once introduced tends to persist. The ritual recitation of parts of the Qur'ān must have favoured this. Again, the revision of an earlier passage, or its occurrence on the back of a sheet that was being used, may sometimes have influenced the choice of expression in a later passage. Further, there are many chance coincidences and curiosities in the use of ordinary words, which might mislead us; and we have to choose as evidence words and phrases which are really characteristic of certain periods or phases of development. It is when we can link the introduction of a characteristic word or phrase to a definite event or turning point of Muhammad's career that it becomes a clear indication of date.

The first question which arises is that regarding the beginning of Muhammad's mission. Tradition has much to say as to the beginning of the revelation. The prevailing tradition is that the first part of the Qur'ān to be revealed was the first few verses of XCVI, 1-5, or perhaps 1-8. This is part of the well-known story of the Call, which represents Muhammad as having been in the habit of going annually to Mt. Ḥirā' to practise what is called *taḥannuth*. The exact significance of this is not explained; it was apparently some sort of pious exercise expressing repentance or doing penance for sin. When, in the fortieth year of his age, he was so engaged, an angel, sometimes specified as Gabriel, came to him with a scroll, and told him to read (or recite). Muhammad replied: "I am not a reader", meaning, probably: "I am not able to read". On being pressed, he answered at last: "What shall I read?" and the angel gave him the words of this passage.

There is, however, another tradition, which seems to have been fairly widespread in early Islam. It gives LXXIV, 1-7 as the earliest passage, and represents Muhammad as having seen a vision of an angel, or, in some versions, a vision of Allah, as he was returning from Mt. Ḥirā' on one or more occasions. Disturbed and terrified by these manifestations, he returned home and asked his wife Khadījah to wrap him in a *dithār*. As he lay thus, the message came to him. This tradition, however, did not prevail against the other, and the usual account combines the two by a sort of conflation. The story of the revelation of XCVI, 1-5 is accepted as giving the earliest passage revealed; but after that there was an interval of two years. LXXIV, 1-7 was then the first passage to be revealed after this interval, which is known as the *fatrah*.

Now, both these passages are in the form of commands to undertake a form of religious activity, and, on the theory that Muhammad's work began with a definite call and commission, are fairly obvious candidates for first place. The supposed mode of their delivery, however, accords rather with later theory than with Muhammad's own early conceptions. It may be questioned if he had any idea of angels to begin with; Gabriel, in particular, is not mentioned in the Qur'ān until Medinan times. The practice of *taḥannuth* is not mentioned at all. The whole story is in fact founded on the nature of the passages themselves combined with the visions which are referred to in LIII, with hints from references in the Old and New Testaments to messages written on scrolls, Ezek. ii, 9 ff., Apoc. x, and from Christian ascetic practice.[1]

[1] I discussed this further in 'Muhammad's Call', *The Moslem World*, XXIV (1934), p. 13 ff.

The visions described in LIII, the reality of which there is no reason to question, do not unfortunately give us any indication of the message laid upon the messenger to deliver. Strictly interpreted, they imply that it was Allah whom he saw, and this seems to presuppose that his mind was occupied at that time with the thought of God rather than with that of the Last Judgment, as is frequently assumed. This agrees with the impression given by the stories of previous messengers, so frequently recounted in the Qur'ān. They were all sent to call their people to the worship of one God. We may then reasonably assume that this was how Muhammad at first conceived of his own mission, and to judge by his later appeals to the Children of Israel, II, 44 ff., and to the Bedouin, XVI, 72 ff., he would begin by stressing the bounty and beneficent power of Allah. His attitude to other gods varied. It would be rash to argue from CVI that he began by summoning his hearers to worship the special god of Meccah, the Lord of the Ka'bah. But Tradition asserts that he did not at first attack the false gods, and this seems very probable. When he did begin to attack them, he did not deny them a certain reality; it is their power to create or to save or to thwart Allah's will that is combated. They were inferior beings of some kind, perhaps associated with the jinn. At one stage, according to the traditional story, he proclaimed that they might be regarded as intercessors with Allah. Later, perhaps about the time of the Hijrah, they were regarded as non-existent; they are mere names which the ancients have invented. Later still, in Medinan times, probably as a reflex of the position assigned by Christians to Jesus, they became real again. They are messengers who have had worship thrust upon them, and will deny their worshippers at the Judgment. It is not always easy to distinguish this point of view from the first.

Muhammad's emphasis on punishment for unbelief came not quite at the beginning, but as a reaction to indifference or opposition. His ideas took two forms. The earlier was that the unbelieving peoples would be overwhelmed by Allah in this world. The later, which developed as the number of believers grew, was Apocalyptic—true believers would enjoy the blessings of Paradise ; for believers who had lapsed, or who did not believe in a future life, there would be the pains of hell. This last idea leads to the introduction of many new terms and phrases (see below, pp. 108-109). It is possible that the angels made their first appearance in connection with the Judgment ; certainly it is in this period that they and, in particular, the Spirit, *ar-rūḥ*, begin to play a part in providence and revelation. These eschatological ideas—which do not altogether displace the idea of the temporal punishment of an unbelieving people—are, in fact, evidence of Muhammad's contact with earlier monotheists and interest in the revelation which had been given them. Of that revelation he seems to have known little to begin with.[1] Such knowledge as he acquires is made available for his followers in the Qur'ān, which confirms what had preceded it (see below, pp. 129, 134). It is probably to this period that the introduction of the name *ar-Raḥmān* for God belongs, and the spiritualising of the sense of *raḥmāh*, ' mercy '. With the spiritualising of the relation of the believers to God and the use of such terms as *tawbah*, ' repentance ', *maghfirah*, ' forgiveness ', *kaffārah*, ' absolution ', and *riḍwān*, ' satisfaction ', we are already in Medinan times.

The removal to Medinah brought Muhammad into close contact with Jews. His attitude was at first friendly, but gradually became hostile. He discovered that the People of the Book would not recognise his teaching. He discovered also that Judaism differed from Christianity. That division among monotheists was a puzzle to him ; passages which discuss it are early Medinan. As a solution to this problem, he fell back upon Islam, ' surrender (to God) ', as the fundamental religion revealed to all the messengers, but afterwards perverted by the presumption and jealousy of their followers. He was thus able to claim a footing for himself as an independent prophet, and for his followers the position of an independent religious community. In thus freeing himself from the tutelage of earlier monotheists he found Abraham,

[1] For a fuller discussion of these statements, some of which may appear controversial, see my *Origin of Islam in its Christian Environment*, Chs. III and IV. Further evidence will appear in the following chapter.

who, neither Jew nor Christian, yet by common consent enjoyed the favour of God, important as a predecessor. He was the ancestor of the Arabs, and the founder of their religion, a *ḥanīf*, one of the *ḥunafā'* or heathen, but no polytheist. His religion Muhammad was to follow.

This important development and turning-point in Muhammad's career, which culminated towards the end of the year II, introduced a number of new ideas, words and phrases which are useful as marks of date. Passages of the Qur'ān which appeal to the testimony of earlier monotheists, or profess to confirm what was previously revealed, are either Meccan or, perhaps more frequently, early Medinan. Those which speak of more than one messenger to the same people show knowledge of Old Testament history and are late Meccan or Medinan. The word *nabīy*, ' prophet ', and most other words derived from Hebrew, are Medinan. Abraham becomes a prophet only in Medinah, and his close association with Ishmael belongs probably to the same time. The word *ḥanīf* and the phrase *millat Ibrāhīm* belong to the period of the change in the year II. *Islām*, *muslim*, and the religious use of the verb *aslama* do not occur before the year II, but once introduced continue to be used. Muhammad's claim to be a prophet belongs to this period, and the use of the word may continue though he shows strong preference for his original title " Messenger of Allah ". Conjoined with this is his claim to receive " the Book ", but " book " has so many uses in the Qur'ān that it has to be used with caution as a criterion of date.

After this crisis there are few changes in the religious teaching of the Qur'ān. The interval between death and the Judgment still caused difficulty. Round about the time of the Hijrah Muhammad was using death as a sanction of his teaching, LXXV, 26 ff., Ibn Hishām, p. 340, leaving it to be inferred that, as the soul was at death, so it would be at the Judgment. Later, those who have died in battle for the cause of Allah are said to be alive, enjoying the favour of God, II, 148 f., III, 163 f. But the idea of the Last Day is retained and the difficulty is not resolved. Fortunately, in the Medinan period Tradition is more reliable, and external events furnish a framework. Some other marks of date may be shortly indicated. All passages which recommend fighting, or speak of the Prophet's followers being engaged in fighting, are necessarily Medinan. So also it was only in Medinah that Muhammad was interested in maintaining the morale of a community. Condemnation of *fasād*, ' corruption ', ' treason ', is thus a mark of the Medinan origin of the passage. *Fitnah*, a word which may have a similar meaning, is too ambiguous to be a safe guide, though probably the majority of its occurrences is Medinan ; similarly with *shiqāq*, ' schism '. Medinan too are the demand to ' obey the messenger ', the conjunction of 'Allah and the messenger ', and the threat of ' humiliation in this world ' directed against opponents, particularly the Jews. The designations applied to opponents vary from time to time. *Kāfir*, ' unbeliever ', with the plural *kāfirīn*, is often used throughout; it is perhaps associated with the initial stress on the bounty of Allah. The other plural, *kuffār*, is prevailingly Medinan. The related verb is *kafara*, ' to be ungrateful ', ' to disbelieve '. Its converse *shakara*, ' to be grateful ', is also general in use, but the participle is not used to designate the Prophet's followers. *Al-mushrikīn*, ' those who ascribe partners ' (to Allah) is a general designation of idolaters at all periods. *Al-mujrimīn*, ' the sinners ', seems to be late Meccan and early Medinan. *Alladhīna kafarū*, ' those who have been ungrateful ' or ' have disbelieved ', is a frequent designation of the Meccans which continues into Medinan times. It is not, however, restricted to them. *Alladhīna ẓalamū*, ' those who have done wrong ', is Medinan and seems to be often applied to the Jews. *Muhājirīn* and *anṣār*, neither of which occurs frequently, are of course Medinan. Uncertain supporters in Medinah were at first referred to as *alladhīna fī qulūbihim maraḍ*, ' those in whose hearts is disease ' ; their conduct at the battle of Uḥud earned them the nickname *al-munāfiqīn*, which from then on practically displaces the other.

ORDER OF THE SURAHS IN VARIOUS CHRONOLOGICAL ARRANGEMENTS

The Roman Numerals give the order in the 'Othmanic Recension; the Arabic ones that in the other arrangements; the numbers in brackets give the verses which are regarded as belonging to a different time from that of the main part of the surah.

'Othmanic	*Muir*	*Noeldeke*	*Grimme*	*Egyptian*
I	6	48	79	5
II	94	91 (parts later a few vv. Meccan)	93 (192-6 later)	87 (281 later)
III	108	97 (parts later)	100	89
IV	107	100	101	92
V	109	114 (parts earlier)	95 (1-14 later)	112
VI	81	89 (91 ?)	89	55 (20, 23, 91, 93, 114, 152-4, Med.)
VII	91	87 (156-8, Med.)	88 (156-8, Med.)	39 (163-9, Med.)
VIII	97	95	97	88 (30-37, Mec.)
IX	114	113	114	113 (129 f., Mec.)
X	79	84	87	51 (41, 94-6, Med.)
XI	78	75	86	52 (15, 20, 116, Med.)
XII	77	77	85	53 (1, 2, 3, 7, Med.)
XIII	89	90	84	96
XIV	80	76 (38-42, Med.)	50 (38-42, Med.)	72 (33 f. Med.)
XV	62	57	48	54
XVI	88	73 (43 f., 111-125, Med.)	83 (111-25, Med.)	70 (126-8, Med.)
XVII	87	67	82	50 (28, 34, 35, 58, 75 - 82, Med.)
XVIII	69	69	81	69 (27, 83-101, Med.)
XIX	68	58	78	44 (59, 72, Med.)

'Othmanic	Muir	Noeldeke	Grimme	Egyptian
XX	75	55	74	45 (130 f., Med.)
XXI	86	65	77	73
XXII	85	107 (1-24, 43-56, 60-65, 67-75, Mec.)	49 (25-42, 76-8, Med.)	103
XXIII	84	64	75	74
XXIV	103	105	98	102
XXV	74	66	73	42 (68-70, Med.)
XXVI	61	56	71	47 (197, 224-8, Med.)
XXVII	70	68	70	48
XXVIII	83	79	69	49 (52-5, Med., 85 on journey)
XXIX	90	81 (1-10, Med., 45 ? 69 ?)	68 (1-12, 45-6, 69, Med.)	85 (1-10, Med.)
XXX	60	74	67	84 (16, Med.)
XXXI	50	82 (13 f., 11-18 ?)	65	57 (26-8, Med.)
XXXII	44	70	64	75 (12-20, Med.)
XXXIII	110	103	108	90
XXXIV	49	85	63	58 (6, Med.)
XXXV	66	86	62	43
XXXVI	67	60	61	41 (45, Med.)
XXXVII	59	50	60	56
XXXVIII	73	59	59	38
XXXIX	45	80	58	59 (53-5, Med.)
XL	72	78	57	60 (58 f., Med.)
XLI	53	71	55	61
XLII	71	83	80	62 (22-4, 26, Med.)
XLIII	76	61	76	63 (54, Med.)
XLIV	58	53	54	64
XLV	57	72	53	65 (13, Med.)
XLVI	64	88	51	66 (9, 14, 34, Med.)
XLVII	95	96	96	95 (14, Mec.)
XLVIII	105	108	112	111

ʿOthmanic	Muir	Noeldeke	Grimme	Egyptian
XLIX	113	112	110	106
L	56	54	47	34 (37, Med.)
LI	63	39 (24 ff., later)	46	67
LII	55	40 (21, 29 ff., later)	45	76
LIII	43	28 (23, 26-33 later)	44 (21-3, 27-33 later)	23
LIV	48	49	43	37 (44-6, Med.)
LV	40	43 (7, 8 later)	42	97
LVI	41	41 (74 ff. ?)	41	46 (70, 71, Med.)
LVII	96	99	102	94
LVIII	98	106	106	105
LIX	102	102	99	101
LX	111	110	105	91
LXI	106	98	104	109
LXII	101	94	94	110
LXIII	104	104	109	104
LXIV	82	93	103	108
LXV	99	101	107	99
LXVI	112	109	113	107
LXVII	42	63	66	77
LXVIII	52	18 (17 ff., later)	38	2 (17-33, 48-50, Med.)
LXIX	51	38	37	78
LXX	37	42	36	79
LXXI	54	51	72	71
LXXII	65	62	52	40
LXXIII	46	23 (20, Med.)	35 (20, Med.)	3 (10, 11, 20, Med.)
LXXIV	21	2 (31-4 later)	34 (55 later)	4
LXXV	36	36 (16-19 ?)	33	31
LXXVI	35	52	32 (30 f. later)	98
LXXVII	34	32	31	33 (48 Med.)
LXXVIII	33	33	30 (37 f. later)	80
LXXIX	47	31 (27-46 later)	29	81
LXXX	26	17	28	24
LXXXI	27	27	27 (29 later)	7
LXXXII	11	26	26	82
LXXXIII	32	37	25	86
LXXXIV	28	29 (25 later)	24 (25 later)	83

'Othmanic	*Muir*	*Noeldeke*	*Grimme*	*Egyptian*
LXXXV	31	22 (8-11 later)	23 (8-11 later)	27
LXXXVI	29	15	22	36
LXXXVII	23	19	21 (7, Med.)	8
LXXXVIII	25	34	20	68
LXXXIX	14	35	19	10
XC	15	11	18	35
XCI	4	16	17	26
XCII	12	10	16	9
XCIII	16	13	15	11
XCIV	17	12	14	12
XCV	8	20	13	28
XCVI	19	1 (9 f. later)	12	1
XCVII	24	14	56	25
XCVIII	100	92	90 ?	100
XCIX	3	25	10	93
C	2	30	9	14
CI	7	24	8	30
CII	9	8	7	16
CIII	1	21 (3 later)	6 (3 later)	13
CIV	10	6	5	32
CV	13	9	4	19
CVI	5	4	3	29
CVII	39	7	2	17
CVIII	18	5	11	15
CIX	38	45	92 ?	18
CX	30	111	111	114
CXI	22	3	1	6
CXII	20	44	91 ?	22
CXIII	92	46	39 ?	20
CXIV	93	47	40	21

All arrangements place surah II as the first of the Medinan surahs.

Muir has therefore		93	Meccan and	21	Medinan
Noeldeke	,,	90	,,	24	,,
Grimme	,,	92	,,	22	,,
Egyptian	,,	86	,,	28	,,

With regard to the Medinan surahs, there is a fair amount of unanimity as to their order, though all the Western scholars recognise that they contain passages of different date. The doubtful surahs are XCVIII, which Muir regards as Meccan, Grimme as doubtfully so, and Noeldeke as Medinan; XXII, which Noeldeke classes as Medinan but with an admixture of Meccan passages. The Westerns divide the Meccan surahs into groups, within which they do not profess that their order is strictly chronological. Muir places 18 surahs before the Call, thus like Noeldeke agreeing with Tradition in regarding XCVI as the surah marking the Call. His other groups are 19-22, 23-41, 42-63, 64-91, 92, 93 (CXIII, CXIV undatable).

Noeldeke's groups are 1-48, 49-69, 70-90. Grimme's, 1-30, CXIII, CXIV doubtfully along with these; 41-50, 51-89; XCVIII, CXII and CIX doubtfully with this group.

CHAPTER VII

STAGES IN THE GROWTH OF THE QUR'ĀN

SIGNS OF ALLAH'S POWER AND BOUNTY

THE view stated above, that Muhammad began by stressing the beneficent power of Allah, leads us, at any rate, to one of the main strands of material which enter into the composition of the Qur'ān. It contains a considerable number of passages in which the phenomena of nature are cited as evidences of God's power, or as instances of the benefits He has bestowed upon men. These are often referred to as 'signs'. Those most frequently cited are: the creation of the heavens and the earth, the creation or generation of man, animals and the various uses and benefits man derives from them, the alternation of night and day, the sun, the moon and the stars, the changing winds, rain (water sent down from the sky), the revival of parched ground, mountains, rivers, the ship running on the sea, vegetation, crops and fruits. Less frequently cited are shadows, thunder, lightning, iron, fire, hearing, sight, understanding and wisdom. In four passages the resurrection is included as one of the 'signs'; II, 26, X, 4, XXII, 65, XXX, 39, all in surahs which admittedly belong to the Medinan or to the late Meccan period. The enumeration of these 'signs' serves various purposes. In some cases they embody a call for gratitude to Allah, XVI, 14, XXX, 45, XXXVI, 73; or for the worship of Him, VI, 102, X, 3. Sometimes they are proofs of Allah's creative power as contrasted with the impotence of the false gods, XVI, 10 ff. Sometimes they are used as evidence of Allah's power to raise the dead, XXII, 5, or to inflict punishment. But taken by themselves, these passages on the whole set before us an idea of an exalted, powerful but beneficent deity. They are not the sort of passages which we should expect to be composed by one whose whole idea of God had been coloured by fear of coming Judgment, and whose religious activity had sprung from the impact of that idea upon him.

These 'sign'-passages occur throughout the Qur'ān and do not belong to any one period of its composition. They form, in fact, one of the means of appealing to men adopted by Muhammad at all stages. In so far as they refer to the permanent objects and constant processes of nature, one would not expect to be able to trace any growth in the list of the 'signs' cited. Gardens and palms, vines and pomegranates were no doubt more common in Medinah than in Meccah, and there are indications that these did not belong to the earliest list of 'signs'. But to argue that passages containing these belong to Medinah, would be going far beyond the evidence. Nor does there seem to have been any fixed list which we can show to have underlain the various passages. As we read them, we acquire a haunting sense of familiarity, of repetition of set-phrases. Thus water is sent down from the sky, II, 20, VI, 99, XV, 22, XVI, 10, 67, etc.; the earth has been stretched out, XIII, 3, XV, 19, L, 7; mountain-peaks have been cast upon it, XIII, 3, XV, 19, XVI, 15, XXI, 32, etc.; the ship runs in the sea; the sun, moon and stars are subdued to service. This may perhaps indicate that the 'signs' have been long in use, and become to some extent stereotyped. But, though we can here and there detect a kind of fixed order, it may at any time be broken through, and the choice of 'signs' cited evidently depends upon the needs and suggestions of the moment.

These passages, then, do not in themselves offer any clear indications of date, apart from the context in which they occur. There are, however, indications that some of them are older than the surahs in which they stand; II, 19b, 20, 26 f., LXXX, 24 ff., LXXXVIII, 17 ff. Many of them have been revised and adapted to their present position, VI, 95 ff., 142 ff., X, 192, XIII, 2 f., 13 ff., XVI, 3 ff., XLI, 37, etc. Occasionally these revisions introduce a reference to resurrection, XXIII, 12 ff., XXXV, 10 ff. The latter passage, like VII, 55 f., brings resurrection into connection with the 'sign' of the revival of dead land by the coming of rain. This illustration of resurrection is peculiarly apt, especially in Arabia, where the effect of rain is almost miraculous. Yet in the majority of verses in which it is referred to, it is simply a token of Allah's bounty or power, without any reference to resurrection ; II, 159, XVI, 67, XXV, 51, XXXII, 27, XXXVI, 33, XLIII, 10, XLV, 4. In several of the passages where it is used to illustrate resurrection there is reason to suspect that there has been revision ; XXX, 47-50, where there is an evident addition in v. 48, and the latter half of v. 49 could be omitted with advantage to the sense ; and XLIII, 10, where a detachable rhyme-phrase seems to have been inserted, as in one or two other verses in the passage. It is evident, at least, that this ' sign ' was used independently of the proclamation of the Last Day and Judgment, though this hardly proves that it was earlier so used. In confirmation of its being early, however, we may note the use of *raḥmah*, ' mercy ', to denote the rain. This word in the context of Judgment and future reward and punishment acquired quite a different sense, and one may question whether, when it had come to be frequently used in this latter sense, it would have been used in the former, had not the ' signs ' already taken shape.

Something similar may be observed in the commonly cited ' sign ' that Allah originates a creature, then restores it, X, 4, 35, XVII, 53, XXI, 104, XXVII, 65, XXIX, 19, XXX, 10, 26, XXXIV, 48, LXXXV, 18. The reference to resurrection is natural, and in the majority of these passages is quite clear. In some, however, it is doubtful, and XXIX, 19 seems to suggest that it originally had no such reference but was based rather on the return of vegetation. So in the recurring phrases, " He giveth life and causeth to die ", and " He bringeth the dead from the living and the living from the dead ", the reference may have been originally to purely natural events.

In some of the other ' signs ', a certain development may be traced. Thus the heaven, or sky, is quite often referred to in the singular as a ' sign '. But where creation is spoken of, we find the plural " heavens and earth ". In some passages we find definitely seven heavens referred to ; II, 27,

XXIII, 17, XLI, 11, LXV, 12, LXXI, 14, LXXVIII, 12. The passage XLI, 8-11 gives an account of creation, in which the earth is created in two days, mountains and foods which the earth produces in four days, and the seven heavens in two days. This may be founded on a vague report of the account of creation in Genesis, i. In other passages creation is said to have taken place in six days; VII, 52, X, 3, etc. (seven passages in all). One has the impression that the Biblical account of creation did not enter into Muhammad's earliest use of the natural signs.

This impression is strengthened by consideration of the references to the production of man. In XCVI, 2 man is said to have been created from *'alaq*, which is usually explained as meaning 'a blood-clot'. Other passages give a fuller account of the natural generation of man, from which it appears that *'alaq* is the earliest discernible stage of the embryo in the womb, XXII, 5, XXIII, 14. It is the wonder of the generation of man that is referred to; XLII, 48 f. So also when man is said to have been created from a drop, XVI, 4, LIII, 47, LXXVI, 2; perhaps also when he is said to have been created from water, XXV, 56. But in other passages man is said to have been created from clay (*ṭīn*), VI, 2, VII, 11, XVII, 63, XXXVIII, 71, 77. In three of these passages the statement is embedded in the story of *Iblīs*, and, as this name seems to be derived from the Greek *diabolos*, one may conjecture that the story and the statement come from a Christian source;[1] cf. the occurrence of the word *ṭīn* in Christian surroundings in III, 43 and V, 110. In XXXII, 6 the creation of man from clay is combined with the production of man "from an extract of water base", cf. XXIII, 12.

In other passages man is said to have been created from dust (*turāb*), III, 52, XVIII, 35, XXII, 5, XXX, 19, XXXV, 12, XL, 69. But in every case, except III, 52, where the position of Jesus is being compared with that of Adam, this is combined with creation from seed, or something similar. All this produces at least a very strong impression that the original 'sign' was that of the natural generation of man,

[1] The Syriac word *ṭīnā* is associated with the creation of man in the simile of the potter, Jeremiah xviii, 6, Romans ix, 21; cf. Qur'ān, LV, 13.

and that the Biblical account of man's creation was later combined with it.

To sum up, then, there are indications that 'sign'-passages, or lists of 'signs', had a more or less independent existence; that they had at first no connection with resurrection and Judgment, but were used to set forth Allah's power and beneficence; and that they were, to begin with, taken from phenomena of Arab experience, and were later combined with ideas derived from Jewish and Christian doctrine. That this was Muhammad's earliest way of appeal to his people cannot perhaps be certainly proved, but a study of these passages corroborates that assumption, and appeals of that kind appear in what are traditionally regarded as very early surahs, as XCVI, 2 ff. CVI is specially worthy of notice. In it the Quraish are urged to serve "the Lord of this House", that is the Kaʿbah, because of the success of their caravan trade, by which he had provided for their sustenance. The designation "Lord of this House" is unique; the nearest parallel is "the Lord of this district" in XXVII, 93. It could hardly have been used while Muhammad was attacking the Meccan gods. To put the surah after the conquest of Meccah and the cleansing of the Kaʿbah from idolatry seems, however, impossible, both on grounds of style and because, at that stage, the ground of the appeal would probably have been different. Tradition, however, says that there was a period at the beginning of Muhammad's mission during which he refrained from speaking against the false gods. One is tempted to regard this surah as belonging to that period, when perhaps he aimed at a revival of the religion which centred round the Kaʿbah.

STORIES OF PUNISHMENT; *AL-MATHĀNĪ*

Consideration of another element in the contents of the Qur'ān leads to similar results. In XV, 87 we read: "We have bestowed upon thee seven of the *mathānī* and the mighty Qur'ān"; and again in XXXIX, 24: "Allah hath sent down the best discourse, a book, self-resembling, *mathānī*, at which the skins of those who fear their Lord do creep, but afterwards their skins and their hearts grow soft to the remembrance of their Lord ". This word *mathānī* has been something of a puzzle to Qur'ān interpreters. The Moslem commentators do not give any satisfactory account of it. It is its proper interpretation, however, rather than the word itself which troubles them. It is an ordinary Arabic plural form, the singular of which would normally be *mathnā*. This form actually occurs in the Qur'ān several times, but always in a sort of adverbial sense ' twofold ', IV, 3, XXXIV, 45, XXXV, 1 ; there is, however, no reason why it should not be a noun meaning ' something doubled ' or ' repeated '. Usually the commentators take *mathānī* in this way, and a favourite interpretation is that it refers to the *Fātiḥah*, which consists of seven verses and is frequently recited in the statutory prayer and elsewhere. Another is that it refers to seven long surahs, of which II-VII are the first six, there being a difference of opinion as to the seventh. In this case the sense of repetition arises from the repeated stories, threats, promises and admonitions which they contain. Sometimes Moslem scholars work with the idea of ' praise ' which is associated with the fourth stem of the same root, and explain that the *Fātiḥah*, or these seven long surahs, are recited to, or contain, the praise of Allah ; the singular of the word would then be *muthnī* or *muthnā*. These interpretations, however, assume a completed and static Qur'ān, and, beyond explaining the number seven, do not suit the implications of the verses in which the word occurs. The suggestion, first made by Geiger, that the word is derived from the Hebrew *mishnāh*, or better, as Noeldeke pointed out, from the Syriac or Jewish-Aramaic form *mathnīthā*, does not give any more satisfactory sense. For, even remembering that not only was the Jewish oral law as a whole called *mishnāh*, but that any particular part of it might be so referred to, the number seven is difficult to account for, and we are still left wondering what it was that was distinct from the Qur'ān, was self-resembling, made the skins of those who feared their Lord creep, and thus by way of fear promoted piety.

Sprenger and several other scholars since his day have taken *mathānī* as a proper Arabic word, in the sense of 'repetitions', and have interpreted it as referring to the stories of punishment contained in the Qur'ān. If we may assume that these stories had at one time a separate existence, the rest of the description would very suitably apply to them. This assumption is indeed to some extent confirmed by the tradition that an-Naḍr, wishing to bring Muhammad into derision, procured stories of the Persian kings, and recited them in opposition to him. Set against most of the contents of the Qur'ān, such rival stories would be quite inept, but if Muhammad were working with these stories of punishment, we see an-Naḍr's point. His stories would be more interesting, and certainly more varied. Muhammad's stories, which are also stories of previous messengers, resemble each other. The general type of them is that a messenger is sent to a people; he delivers his message, but is disbelieved and the message rejected; then the punishment of God falls upon the people for their unbelief. Of such stories there are indeed more than seven referred to in the Qur'ān, but that is not a serious objection, and, as we shall see, they tend to converge upon that number. The list of them is:

1. The story of 'Ād. The name of this people occurs in pre-Islamic poetry, but no definite details are given. According to the Qur'ān, they were a great people of old, perhaps giants, VII, 67, who built 'signs' on eminences, XXVI, 128; their buildings were still to be seen. Whether they are to be identified with Iram of the pillars, mentioned in LXXXIX, 6, is a moot point which depends upon the reading and construction of that passage, and cannot be settled. It is, however, the simplest and most natural interpretation. To them the messenger Hūd was sent; but they disbelieved and were destroyed by a wind which blew for seven nights and days and wiped out everything except the buildings, XLVI, 23 f., LXIX, 6 f.

2. The story of Thamūd. That the Thamūd were a real people of ancient Arabia, there can be no doubt. They are mentioned in an inscription of Sargon, by Ptolemy, Pliny and other classical writers, as well as in pre-Islamic Arab poetry. They seem to have been associated with the North West of Arabia, particularly with al-Ḥijr (Medā'in Ṣāliḥ). Muhammad, probably though not certainly, associated them with this region. They are spoken of as having bored the rock in the wadi, LXXXIX, 6, having built

castles in level places and hewn out the mountain for houses, VII, 72, which seems to be a reference to the remains of buildings and rock-hewn tombs to be found there. Their buildings were still to be seen, XXVII, 53, XXIX, 37. To them a messenger, Ṣāliḥ, one of themselves, was sent, and as a proof of the truth of his message a she-camel and a foal were miraculously produced, which were to be respected and given a share of the water. The Thamūd, however, disbelieved and hamstrung the camel. They were destroyed by an earthquake, VII, 76, by a thunderbolt of punishment, XLI, 16, by a thunderbolt, LI, 44, or by a 'shout' sent upon them, LIV, 31. The unspecified people of XXIII, 32-43, who were destroyed by the 'shout', are probably the Thamūd, if they are to be identified at all, and are not merely a type.

3. The men of al-Ḥijr are probably the Thamūd. Though the tribe and place are never definitely associated in the Qur'ān, in XV, 80-84, the only passage in which they are mentioned, they are said to have hewn out houses from the mountains, and to have been overwhelmed in the morning by the 'shout' for having turned away from the 'signs'. This corresponds to what is said of the Thamūd.

4. The people of Midian. Of them little definite information is given. The only special item in their story is that Shuʿaib, the messenger sent to them, exhorts them to give full measure and just weight, VII, 83, XI, 85 f. Like other disbelieving peoples, they were destroyed—by an earthquake or by a 'shout'.

5. The men of the Grove, referred to in XV, 78, XXXVIII, 12, L, 13, seem, from the only account given of them, XXVI, 176-191, to be identical with the people of Midian, for their messenger is Shuʿaib, and they also are exhorted to give full measure and just weight.

6. The men of ar-Rass are referred to in lists of disbelieving peoples who were destroyed, XXV, 40, L, 12, but no details are given. *Rass* is a word meaning 'well', but it is impossible to identify the place or the people.

7. The people of Tubbaʿ no doubt were a South Arabian people, though the idea that *tubbaʿ* was a title of the kings of Himyar has not been confirmed. They are included in a list of peoples punished for unbelief in L, 13, and are cited in XLIV, 36, but no details of what happened to them are given.

8. Sabā' (Sheba). Whether this is the same people under another name, we cannot say. A long account of Solomon and the Queen of Sheba is given in XXVII, but, as a punishment-story, the fate of Sheba is dealt with only in XXXIV, 14-18, and it does not quite conform to the usual type. No messenger is mentioned as having

been sent to them, but they had a sign given them—two gardens, evidently fruitful. They turned away, and the flood of the dam came upon them and apparently ruined the fertility of their gardens. This is evidently a reference to the bursting of the dam of Ma'rib, which is known to have taken place in A.D. 451 (and again in 542). In the latter part of the story, however, there seems to be a reference to the decay of the Sabaean caravan trade, which is apparently regarded as a punishment for the lengthening of the daily stages to be covered by the caravans.

So far, the stories mentioned seem to be derived from Arab tradition. There are, however, others which carry us into the region of Biblical narrative. Midian, which has been included above, is also Biblical and is in fact mentioned in the Qur'ān in connection with the story of Moses, but there is no hint that the people of Midian, among whom Moses sojourned, were the people whose fate furnished a punishment-story. The account of the fellows of the elephant in CV, which is no doubt derived from some story of an expedition against Meccah, is not really a punishment-story, but rather of the nature of an encouragement to the Prophet. The reference to the fellows of the pit in LXXXV, 1-9 is probably not derived from the story of the persecution of the Christians of Najrān, and in any case has not the form of a punishment-story. The Biblical stories used in this way are the following:

9. Noah. Something may have been known in pre-Islamic Arabia of the story of Noah and the Flood, though the references in early Arab poetry seem doubtful. In the Qur'ān, the people of Noah are frequently referred to as having been destroyed for unbelief. As a developed story it is repeated in some ten places. Usually Noah is sent as a messenger to his people, they disbelieve and are drowned, while he and those who believe are saved in the Ship (Ark). But in some of the passages, particularly in XI, 27-50, the story is expanded so as to include details of the Old Testament story and elements from extra-Biblical Jewish tradition. In another set of passages Noah appears as a prophet, for example IV, 161, and the punishment side of the story falls into the background.

10. Abraham. As a *ḥanīf*, a prophet, and founder of the religion of Abraham, he is frequently mentioned. The story of the visit of the angels to him is related as an introduction to the story

of Lot, XI, 72-78, XV, 51-60, XXIX, 30, 31, and independently in LI, 24-37. This suggests that it was by way of the Lot-story that Muhammad became interested in him. The story of his attacking the idol-worship of his father and people, and, when disbelieved, withdrawing from them is related in XIX, 42-51, XXI, 52-73, XXVI, 69-104, and in XXXVII, 81-96. This last passage comes nearest to the form of a punishment-story, but though his people are twice referred to in lists of earlier unbelievers, who presumably were destroyed, their destruction is never stated. The most that is said is that they were made "the worst losers", XXI, 70, or "the inferior", XXXVII, 96. The story is derived from Jewish tradition.

11. Lot. The story of Lot appears in quite a few passages without any connection between him and Abraham being indicated, VII, 79-82, XXVI, 160-175, XXVII, 55-59, XXXVII, 133-138. In fact, it seems possible that it may have been first derived from local tradition, for in several passages it is indicated that the locality of the story is known and can be seen, XV, 76, XXV, 42, XXXVII, 137. It conforms to the type of the punishment-story in that Lot is said to have been sent to his people. He accuses them of indecency and sodomy. When they oppose and threaten to expel him, he and his household are delivered, all except his wife, who "lingered". The town was then overwhelmed by an evil rain sent upon it, or by a gravel-storm, LIV, 34. When, as already noted, the story becomes associated with the angels' visit to Abraham, it departs from the usual form in that Lot is no longer a messenger to his people, but is troubled when the messengers come to him. In XXIX, 25 Lot is one of those who believe in Abraham, and in XXI, 71 he is delivered along with Abraham, and in v. 74 ff. he is given jurisdiction and knowledge, so becoming a prophet rather than the messenger in a punishment-story.

12. Al-Mu'tafikāt, the overwhelmed cities referred to in IX, 71, LIII, 54, LXIX, 9 are probably to be identified with the cities of the Plain. For in these passages they seem to stand in place of the people of Lot. The Arabic word is probably, as Hirschfeld suggested, adapted from the Hebrew *mahpēkhāh*, which, in the Old Testament, is associated with the destruction of Sodom.

13. Pharaoh is sometimes referred to, without mention of Moses, as an example of one who suffered for his unbelief, for example, LIV, 41 f. In two passages he is described as *dhū l-awtād*, 'possessor of the pegs' or 'stakes', XXXVIII, 11, LXXXIX, 9. What this refers to is unknown. It seems improbable that, as Horovitz suggests, it should refer to his buildings, and there seems to be nothing in Jewish tradition to explain it. It may be that Muhammad had heard of Pharaoh in some other way, but the evidence is

slender. Usually it is the Biblical story of Moses and Pharaoh which lies behind the Qur'ān version. Sometimes it is reduced to the type of a punishment-story, for example in XXIII, 47-50, but more often it is extended to include further details from the Biblical account and others from extra-Biblical Jewish tradition. In some of the versions the punishment of Pharaoh is a mere side-issue, the main object being to give an account of Moses and the Children of Israel.

14. Korah. In XXIX, 38 f. and XL, 24 f. Korah and Haman are associated with Pharaoh. In XXVIII, 76-82 Korah figures as one of the people of Moses who is given great wealth, but being puffed up in pride thereby is destroyed through the earth sinking with him and his dwelling.

Some of these stories (3, 5, 11) appear to be duplicates of others; 6 and 7 are mere references. The story of Sheba is told only once, and that of Korah is evidently an outgrowth of the story of Moses and the Children of Israel. Deducting these, we are left with seven main stories which are repeated and seem to have been used on various occasions. These are the stories of the unbelieving peoples enumerated in XXII, 43, the people of Noah, 'Ād, Thamūd, the people of Abraham, those of Lot, Midian and Moses; all except the last are enumerated in IX, 71 also. These stories occur sometimes singly, sometimes in groups. In particular, there are four passages in which we not only find groups of these stories, but also signs that they have been bound together into a separate composition. In XXVI, 9-191 the seven stories are brought together, and all of them end with the refrain—perhaps a double refrain—"Lo, in that is a sign but most of them have not become believers. But, lo, thy Lord is the Sublime, the Compassionate." Moreover, the last five begin with the formula ". . . counted false the envoys, when their brother . . . said to them", and are otherwise assimilated to each other. The first two, those of Moses and Abraham, not only stand out of their natural order—which is not of much weight—but they differ entirely in their structure and begin in a different way. It looks as if there had been a composition of five stories to which these two have been prefixed. In VII, 57-91 we find these five stories brought together—the story of Moses is recounted at some length in the same surah, but it stands separately, v. 101 ff., and the end of the punishment-stories proper is clearly marked by v. 99 f. Here four of the stories are more or less assimilated to each other, and are bound together by an introductory formula, in which we have to supply the verb from the beginning of the first. The story of Lot falls out of the scheme; not only is it different in form, which might be accounted for by the special nature of the story, but it is introduced in a slightly different way. The same thing appears in XI, 27-98, where these five stories appear in a group; four of them are bound together by the introductory phrase carrying forward the verb used at the beginning, the ends of the stories being also adapted to each other. The story of Lot, to which now the angels' visit to Abraham is prefixed, breaks the connection, though some attempt has been made to close the story in the same way. In LIV, 9-42 we find the four stories, Noah, 'Ād, Thamūd and Lot, bound together by an introductory formula and a refrain; the story of Pharaoh is added as a short reference at the end. Midian does not appear. Another group appears in XXIX, 13-39, though the arrangement is not so clear, additions having apparently been made to the story of Abraham. The stories of Noah, Abraham, Lot and Midian are bound together, followed by references to 'Ād and Thamūd, Korah, Pharaoh and Haman.

It is clear then that Muhammad had a number of such stories which he used sometimes separately, sometimes in groups, and that the groups tend to take a schematised form, the stories contained in them being assimilated to each other by introductory phrases and refrains, and following the same scheme so far as the facts of the story will allow. They are "self-resembling", as the *mathānī* were said to be. XXXIX, 24 implies that these stories were written, and XV, 87 that they were distinct from the Qur'ān.

To some extent we can trace the growth of this main group of stories. Those of Abraham and Moses seem to be the latest additions to it. Whether Lot or Midian was added first may appear doubtful in view of the omission of Midian in LIV, but the series in VII, XI and XXVI, which seem to stand in some relation to each other, imply that Lot was a later insertion into the group. Noah, 'Ād and Thamūd are the constant elements, and are frequently conjoined elsewhere. Whether we can deduce from LIII, 51, where 'Ād is said to have been the first to be destroyed, that the story of Noah had not at that time been used, is doubtful, but it seems probable that Muhammad drew his earliest punishment-stories from Arab, rather than from Biblical, material.

These stories are not given for their narrative or entertainment value. Their purpose evidently is, as we are told that of the *mathānī* was, to soften the hearts of those who heard them by fear of God's punishment and so induce them to accept the message. But they are not stories of eschatological punishment. Resurrection and Last Judgment are hardly mentioned. These do appear in the story of Abraham as given, for example, in XXVI, but this, as we have seen, was a late addition to the series, and there was apparently no tradition of a striking temporal punishment of the people of Abraham. In the version of the stories given in XI the Judgment on the Resurrection-day is tagged on at the end, but evidently the main idea is that the rejection of a divine messenger has in the past brought catastrophe upon the unbelieving people. Nor is the message with which the messenger is charged one of the approaching end of the world and final Judgment. It is consistently one of monotheism, the service of Allah alone. Sometimes there is added the threat of the coming of a "mighty day", but in accordance with the tenor of the stories that is to be interpreted, not as the Last Day, but as the day of Allah's intervention, when a special punishment will fall upon the people if they persist in unbelief.

In the telling of these stories Muhammad adapted them to what was occurring in his own mission. The kernel of the story itself is usually given quite shortly, in such a way indeed as to suggest that it must have been already familiar to his hearers, but the scheme is filled out by variable accounts of what was said by the messenger and by his opponents. In many cases we find these things set down elsewhere as having been said by Muhammad himself and by his contemporaries in Meccah. We are justified therefore in taking these variable parts of the stories as reflecting what happened in his own experience. In one or two places we thus get valuable sidelights on his career. When Ṣāliḥ is said by his opponents to have been one of whom they had good hopes, XI, 65, it may be taken as confirmation of the tradition as to the respected position Muhammad had gained in Meccah before he began his mission. And the account of the plot against Ṣāliḥ, in XXVII, 49 ff., looks like a version of the plot which Tradition says was made to assassinate Muhammad before he left Meccah. The story of Noah as given in LXXI, the earliest part of which is contained in vv. 5-19, seems to be more a version of Muhammad's own experience than an account of Noah. If so, it confirms a tradition (Ibn Hishām, pp. 157, 166), that for some time he carried on his work privately, before he began to "call his people publicly", and it also confirms the supposition that his early appeals were backed by the promise of material prosperity.

Interpreted in this way the punishment-stories imply that Muhammad's message was, in the first place, one of monotheism, and that, at the time when he began to use them, the end of the world and final Judgment played little part in his teaching. The theory behind them is that from each people a messenger is raised up to call them to the worship of the true God, and that the rejection of the message is punished by the destruction of the people. That the messenger and those who believed with him were delivered from the catastrophe, is noted in some of the versions, but not in all. The question, we may surmise, became more pressing as Muhammad became gradually convinced that Meccah was doomed. That only one messenger is sent to each people is clearly implied, if nowhere explicitly stated, X, 48.

THE QUR'ĀN

In XV, 87, quoted on p. 119, the Qur'ān is distinguished from the *mathānī*, and was at that stage apparently separate from them. This is confirmed by other passages in which the Qur'ān is referred to as something distinct and special, V, 101, XVII, 62, etc.

The word *qur'ān* is in fact used in several senses. It is the verbal noun of *qara'a* and is used to denote the act of reading or reciting, XVII, 80, LXXV, 17 f. In a few other places it denotes a single passage recited, X, 62, XIII, 30, and possibly X, 16, LXXII, 1. In most passages in which it occurs, however, the word *qur'ān* seems to refer, if not actually to a book, to some larger whole, a collection of recitations already delivered or in process of being delivered.

This Qur'ān is to be carefully composed, LXXIII, 1-8. It, or at least the idea of it, is 'suggested' by Allah, XII, 3. It is sent down from Allah, IV, 84, XVI, 104, XXVII, 6, LXXVI, 23, and could not have been produced otherwise, X, 38, XVII, 90. It is to be recited by the messenger, X, 62, XVI, 100, XVII, 47, XXVII, 94, LXXXVII, 6 and XCVI, 1, 3 and listened to with respect, VII, 203, XLVII, 26, LXXXIV, 21. It did not come down all at once, but in separate pieces, XVII, 106 f., XXV, 34. High claims are made for it; it is glorious, L, 1, LXXXV, 21, mighty, XV, 87, noble, LVI, 76, clear, XV, 1, XXXVI, 69.

It is evident that the Qur'ān was regarded as being produced under divine behest and guidance, and was given a special position. We must not, however, too readily assume that these laudatory epithets apply directly and simply to Muhammad's own deliverances. When we find them referred to as an Arabic Qur'ān, XX, 112, XLI, 2, etc., it is natural to assume that the Qur'ān might exist in other languages. The verb *qara'a* is probably not native Arabic, and is comparatively seldom used in the Qur'ān, where the usual word for reading or reciting is *talā*. In the Syrian Church the Scripture reading or lesson was designated *qeryānā*, and it is probably from this that the word and the idea were taken. When Muhammad undertook to produce a Qur'ān, he was aiming at giving his followers something similar to the Scripture read in their services by other monotheists. That the Qur'ān was actually so used we know, not only from Tradition, but from the Qur'ān itself, XVII, 80, LXXIII, 20. It was not only similar, but was in fact the same; it reproduced in Arabic for Arabs the revelation which had already been given to others. It confirmed what was before it, III, 2, X, 38, XLVI, 29, and those who had previous revelation in their hands could confirm its truth, X, 94, XVII, 103. Its doctrines were to be found in the Scriptures of the ancients, XXVI, 196, the sheets of Abraham and Moses, LIII, 37, LXXXVII, 18 f. That it agreed with them was a 'sign', an evidence of the reality of the messenger's commission, XX, 133. It, or its message, was "a reminder in sheets honoured, exalted, kept pure, by the hands of scribes, noble and virtuous", LXXX, 11 ff., cf. LVI, 76 ff.

The Qur'ān, then, is the counterpart of the Scriptures used and treasured by earlier monotheists. Its beginning will fall about the same time as the institution of the *ṣalāt*, at any rate after Muhammad had gained some adherents. It marked a new orientation of his religious activity. It is with this, and not with the beginnings of his mission, that the passages traditionally regarded as the earliest in the Qur'ān, are to be associated: XCVI, 1-5, an exhortation to recite, LXXIV, 1-7, a command to rise and warn, LXXIII, 1, 2, 4b-8, an exhortation to compose the Qur'ān carefully, LXXXVII, 1-6, 8, 9, an assurance of aid in reciting. These passages were originally private, but they may be taken as examples of the style in which the Qur'ān was to be composed. The short rhythmic verses with studied rhymes are suitable for memorising and recitation.

The Qur'ān taught what man could not otherwise know, XCVI, 4 f.; it was a weighty word, LXXIII, 5; it was concerned with coming wrath, LXXIV, 5. We may, then, assume the material of its early passages to have consisted mainly of proclamations of coming Judgment, in which, of course, resurrection and punishment and reward in a future life were implied. XC, 1-11, XCII, 1-13 and the *idhā*-passages[1] in general may be taken as examples.

But while the Qur'ān continues to be associated with the idea of warning, it does not remain limited to that. It brings also good tidings to believers, and so we get contrasted pictures of believers and unbelievers at the Judgment, and of the rewards and punishments in store for them, as in LVI and in LXXXVIII, 1-12.[2] It contains all sorts of similitudes and parables, XVII, 91, XVIII, 52, XXX, 58, XXXIX, 28,

[1] See p. 77. [2] For a fuller treatment of this material see the next chapter.

including very elaborate parables, such as XVIII, 31 ff., XXXVI, 12 ff., LXVIII, 17 ff. Further, the Qur'ān guides to what is upright, XVII, 9, and we may find in it moral precepts and even regulations which are more characteristic of a later period. But, meanwhile, Scripture had been found to contain many edifying stories. Of them Muhammad had, up to a point, been negligent, XII, 3. They are now, so far as available, included in the Qur'ān. These stories of religious personalities differ from the punishment-stories ; their point is not the overthrow of unbelieving peoples, but the example and the consequent reward of the prophet or person referred to. Some of them indeed refer to the same persons, but the emphasis is different ; in XXXVII, 73-80 we can see the story of Noah being transformed from the one type to the other. Like the punishment-stories, too, these religious stories tend to be grouped and bound together by introductory phrases and closing refrains, as in XXI and XXXVIII.[1]

It is evident, too, that short didactic-pieces, which might include ' sign '-passages and even an occasional punishment-story, were put together to form longer compositions. The best example is perhaps LXXX, for it consists of five pieces which have clearly been separately composed, but are so arranged that we can follow a line of thought binding them together. In LV and the latter part of LXXVII we have the use of refrain for the same purpose. It was possibly already at this stage that revisions began to be made of earlier passages to adapt them to their position in these compilations, though there were, of course, other reasons for revisions, arising out of changing circumstances and growing experience and insight.

It is probably to these longer compositions that the word *sūrah* came to be applied. It was shortly before or after the Hijrah that the word began to be used, and its occurrence in the first verse of XXIV suggests that it applied to something of this kind. If the derivation of the word suggested above (pp. 51-52) be correct, this would imply that these compositions were written. This is confirmed by the mysterious letters at the head of surahs. Whatever their meaning and purpose,

[1] For the Scriptural material in the Qur'ān see also the next chapter.

they were evidently written symbols, and it was about this same time that they also made their appearance. The earliest of them is perhaps that at the beginning of LXVIII, which is followed by a reference to "the pen and what they write". Others are followed by a reference to the Qur'ān, XX, XXXVI, XXXVIII, L. In XXVII, 1 we find: "These are the signs of the Qur'ān and a book which makes clear". In this and similar formulae it is uncertain whether "these" refers back to the letters or forward to the contents of the surah; further, "book", though usually taken as a reference to the heavenly Book, may simply mean 'a writing'; cf. the beginning of VII, XI and XIV. In XLI we find the letters *ḥā'*, *mīm*, followed by "a revelation from the Merciful, the Compassionate: a book (writing) whose 'signs' have been made distinct as an Arabic Qur'ān"; cf. XV, 1. In other cases the reference to the Qur'ān has disappeared, and it is the Book which is spoken of; in fact, during the period of the use of these letters, the Qur'ān passes over into the Book. In the later portions of our present Qur'ān the word Qur'ān itself is seldom used, and where it does occur it can be taken to mean a closed collection of recitations, as in IX, 112, LXXIII, 20, and in LIV, 17, 22, 32, 40, if these verses be late. The recitation of the Qur'ān is no longer specified as part of the function of the messenger, but has become a part of the ritual of prayer.

There is some evidence that the Qur'ān was definitely closed about the time of the battle of Badr; this corresponds with the great change in Muhammad's attitude to earlier monotheists. It is possible to take the passages above cited as referring to a Qur'ān still in process of delivery, but it is difficult to take II, 181 in that way. The reference there seems to be to a definite sending down of the Qur'ān. This is confirmed by the Moslem interpretation. It takes the phrase defining the period of fasting "the month of Ramaḍān in which the Qur'ān was sent down as guidance for the people and as evidences of the guidance and the *furqān*" to refer to the beginning of the revelation to Muhammad, or more concretely, to the sending down of the heavenly Qur'ān from the presence of God to the nearer heaven so as to be available for transmission to him. There are other passages in which, though the Qur'ān is not specifically mentioned, reference seems to be made to the sending down of something as a whole at a definite time, XLIV, 2 : "We have sent it down on a blessed night" ; XCVII, 1 : "We have sent it down on the night of power (or decision)" In VIII, 42 we find reference to something having been sent down "on the day of the *furqān*, the day the two parties met". This clearly designates the day of Badr and associates it with the *furqān*. Remembering that the battle of Badr took place in the month of Ramaḍān, we seem to be led to the conclusion that it was for this reason that that month was ordained as the period of fasting, and that what was sent down was some form of the Qur'ān. That something of the sort was in preparation is perhaps indicated by XX, 113, where the Prophet is admonished not to be in a hurry with the Qur'ān. Possibly it was a written form of it which was now produced as "evidence of the guidance and the *furqān*". This would explain also the association of *furqān*, which is probably derived from Syriac *purqānā*, 'salvation', with Scripture.[1] It might also be the "preserved tablet", cf. LXXXV, 21 f. These arguments are, however, precarious, and the conclusion to which they point is difficult to reconcile with the complete absence in Tradition of any mention of such a written form of the Qur'ān. It may be urged in explanation of this silence that the *furqān*, of which this sending down of the Qur'ān was an evidence, played only a passing rôle in Muhammad's ideas. Only once is it explicitly said to have been sent down to him, XXV, 1, and once this is probably implied, III, 2. There is no mention of it in the later Medinan portions of the Qur'ān. Still, it is strange that what seems to have some importance, though a passing one, left no trace in Tradition.[2]

[1] See note on *al-furqān* (pp. 136-138).

[2] The following tentative list of passages and surahs, the basis of which belongs to this period, may be given: XCVI, 1-8, LXXIV, 1-7, LXXXVII, 1-9, LXXIII, 1-8, XC, 1-11, CII, XCII, XCI, 1-10, LXXX, LXVIII, XCIX, LXXXII, LXXXI, 1-14, LXXXIV, 1-6, 7-12, C, LXXIX, LXXVII, LXXVIII, LXXXVIII, LXXXIX, LXXV, LXIX, LI, LII, LVI, LXX, LV, LIV, XXXVII, XLIV, L, XX, XXVI, XV, XXXVIII, XXXVI, XLIII, XXVII, XIV, XII, XXXIX, XLII, X. XIII. The surahs are quoted in Noeldeke's order.

THE BOOK

Whether or not the Qur'ān came to a definite close, its place is ultimately taken by the Book. We have seen this happening in the beginnings of surahs. Epithets which had been originally applied to the Qur'ān come to be applied to the Book. Here, too, we have to remember that these epithets may not apply directly to a book given to Muhammad. For, by this time, the Book had become a designation for revelation in general.[1] But it is clear that what was sent down to Muhammad came to be designated as *kitāb*, 'writing', rather than as *qur'ān*, 'recitation'. That he contemplated producing a book or writing of some sort appears from the first half of XIX, where each section begins with the phrase: "Mention in the Book . . ." So we find in a number of passages that the Book has been sent down to him, III, 2, 5, IV, 106, V, 52, XVI, 66. Some of these passages may possibly be interpreted as meaning merely that knowledge of the heavenly Book had been bestowed upon him, but in others it is clear that a Book has actually come to him. Thus in II, 83 a Book has come from Allah confirming what people already had; so too in VI, 92, XLVI, 11, 29. V. 48-55 makes it pretty clear that something similar to the Torah and the Evangel was meant.

This was in accord with the situation which had developed after the Hijrah. In his new position as head of a band of refugees and mediator between hostile sections of the Medinan population, mundane matters were claiming more of the Prophet's attention, and his deliverances were taking wider scope. His knowledge of the nature and contents of the revelation cherished by Jews and Christians had become clearer, and was expanded by the close contact with Jews into which he was now brought. The Qur'ān, as he had at first conceived it, no longer quite corresponded to what he now knew the Book to be. Nor were the appeals, exhortations and regulations which his position now demanded of him suitable for inclusion in a Qur'ān intended primarily

[1] For a treatment of this idea see next chapter.

for recitation. Besides, in the controversy which had developed, especially with the Jews, his own position had changed. His sense of prophetic mission had intensified. He had become the leader and guide of an independent religious community, and it was essential that that community should, like the others, have its Book. The need had been perhaps temporarily supplied by the special Qur'ān, but something wider and more inclusive seemed now demanded.

This points to the early Medinan period as the time when the Book was begun. The line between Qur'ān and Book need not be drawn too decidedly, for, in view of their somewhat different nature, the two may have overlapped a little in time. Surah II which, after an introduction, starts with the story of Adam and then goes on to appeal to the Children of Israel, and was probably intended to be the beginning of the Book, shows that some at least of the material was produced fairly early in Medinah, before the break with the Jews was complete. But, of course, when the arranging had commenced, earlier material would naturally be included.

The Book was never completed, and if it was ever planned in any logical form, which is doubtful, the plan was continually broken in upon by the necessities of a community fighting for its life against external opposition and ever calling for legislation to regulate its internal affairs and govern its social life. The form in which it was left is probably much that of our present Qur'ān; the redactors of the time of ʿOthman may have arranged the order of the surahs, but seem otherwise to have followed what they found in the *ṣuḥuf* as closely as possible. If this be so, and if we can take the present Qur'ān as representing the Book, it is evident that it was intended to include all the kinds of material which had come to him in the course of his mission. 'Sign'-passages had probably already been included in the Qur'ān; others may have been adapted for inclusion in the Book. The groups of punishment-stories in VII and XI show traces of Medinan revision, which suggests that these stories also were adapted for the same purpose. We cannot, of course, say definitely whether the Medinan additions to early passages were made for the purpose of including them in the Book or in order to recite them anew in Medinah. For it is evident that some pieces were used again after revision, just as deliverances made in Medinah were revised in the light of experience or of the needs of some similar situation. But the two openings to surah XII show that that surah, which had been recited as part of the Qur'ān, was revised and extended for inclusion in the Book. The variation in rhyme in XIII and XIV argues that material put together for one purpose was afterwards revised and added to for another, so that we may expect to find later additions even in surahs which had belonged to the Qur'ān in the special sense. The Book was, in fact, to be the complete revelation, including natural signs, punishment-stories, Qur'ān, and any further deliverances which might from time to time be 'suggested'.

NOTE ON *AL-FURQĀN*

The word *furqān* occurs seven times in the Qur'ān: II, 50, 181, III, 2, VIII, 29, 42, XXI, 49, XXV, 1. Its use is difficult to explain, and various suggestions have been made as to its derivation. For a discussion of these, reference may be made to Jeffery: *Foreign Vocabulary*, p. 225 ff., who favours derivation either from the Syriac *purqānā* or from the Jewish-Aramaic *purqān*. Something will depend on the date at which the word was introduced. In *The Origin of Islam* I assumed that XXI and XXV were Meccan and that the word was introduced when Muhammad was occupied with the deliverance of believers from the temporal catastrophe which he had proclaimed would fall upon an unbelieving community. I am now inclined to think that the word belongs to about the time of Badr. So far as Muhammad and his followers are concerned, the giving of the *furqān* cannot be earlier than that. VIII, 29 clearly implies that no *furqān* had yet been given them; for it is a promise that one will be given them if they believe. This promise was evidently fulfilled at the time of Badr, which is referred to as "the day of the *furqān*", VIII, 42. The mention of the *furqān* in III, 2 and XXV, 1 must therefore be later than Badr. II, 50, in which the Book and the *furqān* are said to have been given to Moses, belongs to the time when Muhammad was still appealing to the Jews and must, though Medinan, be considerably earlier than Badr. XXI, 49, in which the *furqān* is given to Moses and Aaron, and is associated with illumination and the reminder, probably belongs to about the same time. The association of Aaron with Moses suggests that v, 28 may have some relevance here and throw light on Muhammad's interpretation of the term. This passage, which recounts the refusal of the people of Moses to enter the Holy Land if it involved fighting, ends with Moses' appeal : "O my Lord, I control no one but myself and my brother ; make a separation (*fa-fruq*) between us and the reprobate people ". According to II, 48-50 it was at Sinai, after the incident of the golden calf, that Moses received the Book and the *furqān*. In the passage VII, 142 ff., which tells of the giving of the tablets (*alwāḥ*) to Moses, his return to find that his people had meanwhile set up a calf to be worshipped, his upbraiding of Aaron, and the latter's excuse and appeal not to be placed with the wrong-doing people, we find Moses again praying: "O my Lord, forgive me and my brother and cause us to enter into Thy mercy " (v. 150), and this is followed by the declaration of the different treatment to be accorded to "those who took the calf" and "those who have done evil deeds and then thereafter have repented and believed ". There is, indeed, no mention of the *furqān* here, or any use of the Arabic root *faraqa*, 'to separate'. But there is, in fact, a separation made between those who are accepted of God and those who are not ; and v. 155, with its curious use of the root *hūd*, seems to imply that this was, in Muhammad's mind, the origin of the Jews, *Yahūd*, as a distinct religious community.

In the period before Badr Muhammad had been breaking away from the Jews and the Christians and setting up his followers also as a distinct religious community. We can imagine that they, exposed to the taunts of Jews and Christians alike, who both claimed to have assurance of divine acceptance based in each case on a deliverance, were a little uneasy that they had no such assurance, no *furqān*. This seems to be the situation which is met in VIII, 29 ; we may note that there the *furqān* is associated with absolution from evil deeds and forgiveness. This gives a slight presumption that it was from Christian sources that the word was derived, but Muhammad must have associated it with the Arabic root *faraqa*, 'to separate', and taken it to imply the separation of an accepted religious community from the unbelievers. This was associated also, as in the case of Moses, with the giving of a distinctive revelation. The Jews had the Torah, and the Christians had the Evangel ; so now the Moslems have the Qur'ān as their form of the Book ; III, 2, IX, 112.

The victory at Badr was not only a 'deliverance' of the small band of Moslems who had gone out with Muhammad expecting to intercept a caravan and had found themselves face to face with an army. It was a final separation between Muhammad's followers and the unbelieving Meccans; after the bloodshed which had taken place there could be nothing but enmity. It was also a sign of the acceptance of the Moslem community in Allah's eyes, and of the rejection of the unbelievers, III, 10 f. If we may take XLVIII, 1 ff. in this connection, it meant a new assurance on Muhammad's own part, an assurance of the forgiveness of sins. There is some ground for this, for the *fatḥ*, 'clearing-up', which is there said to have been given him, is in VIII, 19 definitely associated with Badr. All this confirms the suggestion that the choice of the month of Ramaḍān as the period of fasting was due to the victory having been won in that month. II, 181, which ordains the fast, says that in that month the Qur'ān was sent down as guidance for the people and as evidences of the guidance and the *furqān*; in VIII, 42 something is said to have been sent down on the day of the *furqān*, the day the two parties met—a clear reference to the day of Badr. Here, then, we have the appearance of the Qur'ān as the distinctive Scripture of an independent Moslem religious community, linked with the *furqān*, the separation of believers from unbelievers, and the assurance of forgiveness and acceptance with God; and both linked with the day of Badr.

CHAPTER VIII

CONTENTS AND SOURCES OF THE QUR'ĀN

TEACHING

No man can entirely divest himself of the ideas of his youth. It was only natural that some of the primitive ideas of Arab paganism should have clung to Muhammad, and should appear in the Qur'ān. The jinn, those eerie spirits by which the primitive Arab felt he was surrounded, are regarded as real beings, though it is denied that they can be of use to man in discovering secrets. Shooting stars are interpreted as heavenly projectiles launched to drive away the jinn and prevent them gaining knowledge of secrets by listening to the deliberations of the High Council.[1] Such matters are unessential. More characteristic of the Qur'ān is the reaction from pagan ideas. It was Muhammad's life-work to overthrow the polytheism of his people. Some of the pagan deities are referred to by name. The idea that the goddesses are the daughters of Allah, and that Allah should have female offspring, while men have male children, is ridiculed. The food taboos of paganism are rejected, as well as the related custom of sacrificing animals on stone altars, probably regarded as representing the deity. The practice of burying female infants alive was condemned and abolished. On the other hand, some of the practices of the pre-Islamic Arabs were adopted, in a modified form no doubt, into Islam. Thus the pilgrimage, the visiting of the Ka'bah and circling round it, and the reverence paid to the Black Stone which is built into its wall, were pre-Islamic practices. The law of retaliation was adopted, modified by the proviso that the injury inflicted must not exceed the injury received, and by the recommendation that it was better and more meritorious to forgive the injury altogether. In fact, after his quarrel

[1] See p. 144.

with the Jews, Muhammad regarded it as his function to purify the Arab religion and restore it to its primitive monotheism. The deliberate incorporation of Arab practices belongs to that period.

The interest of Western scholars has naturally been concentrated more on those elements of the Qur'ān which show kinship with Judaism and Christianity. That it contains much Biblical material is evident at a glance, and we have seen that the Book which was in the hands of Jews and Christians attracted much attention from Muhammad. The difficulty he appears to have had in obtaining a correct idea of the nature and contents of the Scriptures forbids us to conceive of Muhammad as having been in close contact with either Jews or Christians before the beginning of his mission. That he borrowed largely in the course of that mission is acknowledged. In fact, the claim to produce an Arabic Qur'ān and to confirm the Scriptures which were before it, shows that he consciously aimed at reproducing the main part of these Scriptures. But this direct borrowing of Biblical, or what he believed to be Biblical, material belongs mainly to his late Meccan and early Medinan period. Later, the knowledge which he had acquired of Jewish and Christian doctrine and practice no doubt influenced his teaching and regulation of his community, but again in a more or less indirect way. Muhammad, in truth, occupies a more independent position than has usually been allowed to him. He is also an independent personality, not perhaps an original thinker, but a reflective man in close contact with the realities of life, who put his own stamp even on his borrowings.

The Idea of God.—The fundamental doctrine of the Qur'ān is that there is only one God. From that doctrine Muhammad never wavered from start to finish of his mission, except perhaps on the one occasion when he was tempted to compromise with the Quraish by acknowledging other beings as intercessors with Allah. For the most part it is directed against the polytheism of his own Arab people. To associate other beings with Allah in worship is the deepest offence to Allah, and is at the same time stupid and unintelligent. At a later stage in Medinah, when he came into direct contact with Christianity, he was equally uncompromising towards the Christian doctrines of the Sonship of Christ and of the Trinity, the worship of Jesus and the veneration of the Virgin Mary. He never understood the doctrine of the Trinity ; if he had, he might have tempered somewhat the baldness of his conception of God, but it must be admitted that in the beliefs and practices of the Christians with whom he came into contact, there was probably justification for his protest.

Characteristic of God is the power to create. The false gods have created nothing. " They (the unbelievers) have taken, apart from Him, gods who have created nothing, but are themselves created ", XXV, 3. " Say: 'Have ye considered what ye call upon apart from Allah? Show me any part of the earth that they have created, or have they a share in the heavens?' ", XLVI, 3. " Those whom ye call upon apart from Allah will not create a fly, even if they join together to do it ", XXII, 72. There cannot be any god apart from Allah, for then " each god would go off with what he had created, and set himself up against the others ", XXIII, 93.

As to the nature of the false gods, the statements of the Qur'ān vary somewhat. Prevailingly they are regarded as being nothing at all. " They neither profit nor hurt ", XXV, 57. " They are not able to help themselves ", XXI, 44. They are designated *al-bāṭil*, 'the vain thing', XXIX, 52. People take their own desire as a god, XXV, 45. " What ye worship apart from Allah are only names which your fathers have named ", XII, 40. The polytheists will be asked on the Resurrection-day where their gods are, XVI, 29. They will call for them but will receive no answer, XVIII, 50. At other times a certain reality is assigned to these gods. In one passage they are said to be jinn, VI, 100; in another the polytheists are said to worship a rebellious Satan, IV, 117. In another the gods go to Gehennah along with their worshippers, XXI, 98, 99. In others, while actually present at the Judgment, they repudiate any responsibility for the worship offered them, X, 29 f., XXV, 18*f*. These latter passages perhaps refer to messengers, such as Jesus, to whom their followers have offered worship.

In contrast to them, Allah is the one who creates, XCVI, 1, 2. He is the creator of everything. He is the creator of the heavens and the earth and what is between them. Everything therefore belongs to Him. Man may have a certain power over things on the earth, he is *khalīfat Allāh* on the earth, but Allah is the owner of all power; He gives it to whomsoever He wills and takes it from whomsoever He wills, and in the end all things return to Him; He inherits everything. Allah is able to do anything. When He decides upon a thing He simply says "Be", and it is. All things in heaven and earth are His creatures.

Allah being the creator of all things, the good things of life are His gift. He gives freely to some, to others He measures things out, but no one can complain of being wronged. He has a claim to gratitude from man, and the sign of gratitude is to acknowledge Allah as God and worship Him. Not to do so is *kufr*, properly 'ingratitude', but thus coming to mean 'unbelief'.[1] The word which has come to be used for the name of the religion which Muhammad founded, Islam, does not make its appearance until Medinan times, but it too springs from the idea of Allah's power, and man's dependence. Islam is the surrender of oneself to Allah's will made known in revelation.

No doubt there is some measure of development in the idea of God, but fundamentally it remains the same all through. What change there is, is in the direction, first, of increasing realisation of the sublimity of Allah and of the spiritual nature of His good gifts and His mercy, and, second, of stressing the arbitrary power of Allah at the expense of His benevolence. The idea of arbitrary predestination hardens, as was perhaps natural in the course of the stern struggle which the Prophet had to carry his religion to success, but the bounty and goodness of Allah are never dropped out of sight entirely.

That is the aspect of Allah's character which was stressed at the beginning. It is the one which lies behind the

[1] Cf. *kafara'* p. 109.

' sign '-passages. Tor Andrae has sought to make out that this material is Christian, but he assumes a direct bearing of these ' signs ' upon the resurrection, which is not present in the Qur'ān, or appears only in the later ' sign '-passages. The essential function of the ' signs ' in the Qur'ān is to inculcate the power and bounty of Allah, and they relate too closely to Arab conditions to have been directly borrowed from outside. This theistic use of them was, no doubt, derived from the influence of Judaism and Christianity upon Arabia. But the question which of these religions had more influence on Muhammad to start with is really the question which of them had contributed more to form that atmosphere, presumably fairly widespread, of dissatisfaction with polytheism.

The derivation of the name Allah is not quite certain. Wellhausen suggested that it was a contraction for *al-ilāh*, ' the god '. Each tribe would refer to its own god as ' the god ', and hence the name. Others hold that it is the Syriac *alāhā*, and to this I would myself incline, but as the name was in use in Arabia in pre-Islamic times, that proves nothing as to the derivation of Muhammad's monotheism. The other proper name which is given to God, namely, *ar-Raḥmān*, also seems to have been in use in Arabia before Muhammad's time. It has been found in South Arabian inscriptions, and it was used by other prophets who appeared in Arabia towards the end of Muhammad's life. The form may be Jewish; it seldom occurs in Syriac, and is common in Jewish writings; but Muhammad's direct dependence on Judaism for its adoption is very doubtful. It is a quite regular Arabic form. In any case, it hardly belongs to the earliest parts of the Qur'ān. Its introduction is no doubt associated, as Grimme held, with the stress which is laid in the later Meccan period on God's *raḥmah*, ' mercy ', which is conceived in a much more spiritual sense than the earlier use of the word implies. This is an element of the gentler and richer idea of God which appeared, partly under stress of failure and persecution and partly as the result of growing knowledge of earlier Scripture, towards the end of the Meccan period, and continued, for the believers at least, to temper the sternness of God's arbitrary power which had become prominent in Medinan times. Whether it was through Jewish or Christian channels that this mellowing influence came, we do not know. As Grimme says, however, it was in Christianity that the idea of the love of God had been given most prominence, and there is other evidence that it was through Christian channels that knowledge of the Scriptures was coming to Muhammad at this stage.

Other Spiritual Beings.—Angels do not appear in the earliest parts of the Qur'ān; they belong to the period of closer contact with Judaism and Christianity. If we judge by the form of the word *mal'ak*, and especially by its plural *malā'ikah*, it is a borrowing from Ethiopic, and thus reached Muhammad from Christian sources. But it seems probable that the word was known to the Arabs before his time, though unlikely that pagans were so interested in the idea as to demand that an angel should have been sent as messenger, XLI, 13, or in company with him, XLIII, 53. The nature of the High Council is not clear. In XXXVII, 8 it belongs to a piece of pagan mythology, but in XXXVIII, 69 it seems to denote the angels to whom Allah made known His intention to create man, cf. verse 71. Another question, difficult to answer, is, who were the people who held the angels to be female, XXXVII, 150, XLIII, 18, or gave them female names, LIII, 28? We seem to be driven to assume that some pagans had adopted the idea of angels, or that Muhammad himself represented the worship of goddesses as worship of supposed female angels.

The angels are subordinate and created beings, XXI, 26; they are messengers, XXXV, 1; they surround the throne and sing the praises of Allah, XL, 7, XLII, 3; on the Judgment-day they will be seen, II, 206, XXXIX, 75, LXIX, 17; their coming would betoken that the end was at hand, XV, 8; being part of 'the affair of Allah' they become watchers over men, and recorders of their deeds, XIII, 12, LXXXII, 10 f.; they call in the souls of men at death, XVI, 30, 34; they become also the medium of revelation, a function which falls specially to Gabriel, II, 91, LXXXI, 19 ff. The only other angel mentioned by name is Michael, II, 92.

The Spirit also belongs to 'the affair of Allah', XVII, 87; like the angels, it will appear at the Judgment, LXXVIII, 38; the angels bring it to whomsoever God wills, evidently as part of the inspiration of a prophet, XVI, 2, XL, 15. Thus it is implanted in Muhammad, XLII, 52, and, probably as an intermediate step, becomes like Gabriel the bearer of the Qur'ān, XXVI, 193. This is, no doubt, a development of Old Testament ideas. Where Jesus is said to be supported by the spirit of holiness, II, 81, 254, V, 109, Christian ideas no doubt form the background. Allah's spirit is breathed into Maryam (the Virgin Mary), XXI, 91, and Jesus is said to be a spirit from Him, IV, 169. But no clear idea emerges either of the prophetic spirit or of the spirit of holiness.

At the other end of the scale are the satans who, in many respects, resemble the jinn and perhaps took their place, LXVII, 5. They are, however, of the tribe of Satan, VII, 26, and prompt men to evil, XIX, 86, XXIII, 99. They are assigned to unbelievers as mates, XLI, 24, XLIII, 35, just as the angels are the guardians of believers.

Satan, *ash-Shaiṭān*, the great enemy of mankind, belongs to the Jewish and Christian thought-world. To judge by the form of the word, it and the idea came through Ethiopic Christian channels. A Christian origin is also indicated by the name *Iblīs*,[1] which in some narratives takes the place of *ash-Shaiṭān*. He is an angel, deposed for his pride in refusing to do obeisance to man at his creation, II, 32, XV, 28 ff. He is respited and given permission to tempt men from the straight path. He has, however, no real authority over them. He makes their deeds seem fair to them, VIII, 50, XVI, 65, but urges to evil and unseemliness, II, 164. He whispers in the breasts of men, VII, 19, XX, 118, CXIV, 4 f., and may even insinuate something into the deliverances of prophets, XXII, 51. His footsteps are not to be followed, for he is a betrayer of men, XXV, 31, and will repudiate their service at the last, XIV, 26 f.

The Prophet.—Muhammad's doctrine of the messenger or prophet is coloured by his own experience. At first, he is simply a messenger to his own town. Other messengers had

[1] See p. 118.

been sent before him. Each had been sent to his own people to call them to the worship of the one God and to warn them of the consequences of unbelief. It has been suggested that this idea of a messenger to each community, bringing to each the same message, is derived from, or has kinship with, Manichaean ideas. But it hardly seems necessary to go so far for the idea of *rasūl Allāh*. Anyone sent on a commission from one to another was, in Arabia, a *rasūl*. If Muhammad felt himself impelled to advocate the worship of the one God, Allah, he would very naturally claim to be the Messenger of Allah. The idea of similar messengers having been sent to earlier communities needs no further explanation than the inquiring mind of a man who found himself disbelieved, and looked round for material to impress upon his people the danger and disastrous effects of unbelief.

Without altogether displacing this simple idea of the messenger, contact with Biblical ideas gave the message a wider application; it became "a reminder to the worlds", VI, 90, LXVIII, 52. But though Muhammad's message became implicitly universal, he continued to deal almost exclusively with the people with whom he was in contact. He never lost his foothold in the actual world. His own experience of divine prompting is the key to his understanding of the prophets; but there is a progressive interaction between his interpretation of his experience and mission, and the conception of the prophet which he learned from Jews and Christians. At first he seems to have conceived that the prompting came from Allah in person. Then, probably under the influence of the Old Testament idea of the Spirit which came upon the prophets, he interprets his experience as caused by a spirit implanted in him by Allah, XLII, 52. Finally, it is the angels who are the bearers of revelation, and it is Gabriel in particular who brings it down upon his heart, with Allah's permission, II, 91. Messengers, however, are always human beings; they eat and drink and have wives and children, XIII, 38. If the inhabitants of the earth had been angels, an angel would have been sent, XVII, 97. As they are men, messengers have been, like himself, men to whom 'suggestions' have been made, XII, 109, XVI, 45,

XXI, 7. They came of the people to whom they were sent and used their language. They wrought no signs, except by permission of Allah. They were concerned only with the proclamation, the delivery of the message with which they were charged, and had no authority over their people, or responsibility for their unbelief. Under the influence of Jewish and Christian ideas, however, and especially the story of Moses, the messenger or prophet, *nabīy*, as in early Medinan times he came to be called, assumed higher status. He is sent to be obeyed, IV, 67 ; he is given the Book that he may judge amongst the people, IV, 106. To be given the Book is the prerogative of a prophet, XIX, 31, and jurisdiction goes with it, III, 73, VI, 89. He is a witness over his people, II, 137. That he will have a right of intercession for his people is not stated, but it is left open that he may be given permission to intercede.

The prophetic office is thus a high distinction and a high favour bestowed upon a man or a prophet. In this respect the Children of Israel have been specially favoured, XLV, 15. The early idea that one messenger was sent to each people was modified by the knowledge that to them more than one had been sent. This enabled Muhammad to free himself from the leading-strings of Judaism and Christianity by adopting the religion of Abraham. For Abraham, who, to begin with, was the hero of a punishment-story, became in early Medinan times a prophet, a *ḥanīf*, the founder of the religion of the *ḥunafā'* or heathen, and this religion it is Muhammad's task to restore to its pristine monotheism. The prophetic office then comes to be not only the privilege of a special people, but resides in a special family, the descendants of Abraham, XXIX, 26, LVII, 26. " Verily Allah hath chosen Adam and Noah, the family of Abraham, and the family of 'Imrān above the worlds ; descendants one of the other ", III, 30. The family of Abraham would no doubt include Muhammad himself, Abraham being the ancestor of the Arabs ; and the family of 'Imrān would include Moses and Jesus. These then are given preference over others. But there are others of whom lists are given, VI, 84 ff., XIX, 52ff., XXXVII, 73 ff.

The source of all this is evidently the Scriptures, mainly the Old Testament, or rather the knowledge of Scripture mediated to Muhammad by Jews and Christians with whom he came into contact, and understood by him in the light of his own situation and needs. Ahrens (*Muhammed*, p. 130) finds in the lists of prophets which the Qur'ān contains evidence of the influence of Gnostic Christianity, but the lists which he quotes from such Christian sources do not correspond to any list in the Qur'ān. The Qur'ān lists are really the result of a painful process of gathering information and gradual sifting of it into some sort of shape, a process which we can trace in the Qur'ān itself. The list of those chosen, for example in VI, 84 ff., is not a list made out by anyone familiar with the Bible or borrowed from a literary source, but that of one who had been inquiring as to the names of Biblical persons, and had noted down for future use some of the names given to him. We do not need to assume Mandaean influence to account for John the Baptist being recognised as a prophet and spoken of as receiving the Book. Any Christian informant might call John a prophet, and that title would to Muhammad's mind imply that he had been given the Book. Nor do we need to seek for obscure influences to account for the fact to which Tor Andrae calls attention, that the great writing-prophets of the Old Testament are not even mentioned by name. This does not mean that Muhammad was drawing his information from some obscure circles who regarded written prophecy as excluded. The explanation is much more simple. The prophetic books of the Old Testament are unfortunately not easy to read; even today, the ordinary man—even the ordinary Christian—knows little about them. Muhammad's informants either did not know of them or forgot to mention them. There is no objection to written prophecy in the Qur'ān.

The Revelation.—We have seen that until, in Medinah, he discovered that the Jews did not accept his message, but were hostile to him, Muhammad regarded himself as reproducing for his own Arab people the revelation which had previously been given to others. What was sent down to him confirmed what was before it. He at first conceived this as a Qur'ān, something to be read or recited in worship, dealing with the Last Things, Resurrection, Judgment, and Future Life. In particular, it is Judgment to come which is the main burden of his early *qur'āns*. For this reinforced, and in a way took the place of, the catastrophe which in the punishment-stories fell upon the unbelieving people. He is a warner and his message continues to be a warning.

It is this sense of warning that lies behind the designation of it as a *tadhkirah*; LXIX, 48, LXXIII, 19, LXXVI, 29, etc., *dhikrā*, VI, 68, 90, XI, 116, 121, LXXIV, 34, etc., and as *dhikr*, XII, 104, XXXVIII, 87, LXVIII, 52, LXXXI, 27, etc. These, however, are not technical words, but may be used in other senses. In some passages *dhikr* has obviously the sense of private or public worship or prayer, II, 196, V, 93, LXII, 9, LXIII, 9. Words from the cognate roots are used both in Hebrew and in Syriac to denote parts of, or kinds of, religious service. But it seems unnecessary to suggest borrowing. According to the common meaning of the verb *dhakara*, the phrase *dhikr Allāh* or *dhikr ar-Raḥmān* may mean either man's 'remembrance of God', or 'God's remembrance of' or 'reminder to' man. The former sense, that is, worship or prayer, is found mostly in Medinan passages; the latter is the earlier sense. Anything which reminds man of God may be a *tadhkirah*, LVI, 70 ff., LXIX, 12, or a *dhikrā*, L, 8, 36. The coming of a messenger may be a reminder, but usually it is the message which is designated *dhikr*, VII, 61, 67, etc. Previous revelation was of the nature of *dhikr*; those who possess it are *ahl adh-dhikr*, and the Qur'ān, which contains a similar message, is *dhū dh-dhikr*, XXXVIII, 1.

It corresponds to this early conception of the revelation as reading or recitation that the first part of Scripture to be mentioned by name is the Psalter, *az-zabūr*. The name is difficult to account for; it possibly arises from a confusion of Hebrew *mizmōr* with the Arabic root *zabara*, 'to copy', 'transcribe', and seems to have been in use before Islamic times. The plural *zubur* is used in the general sense of Scriptures in XXIII, 55, XXVI, 196, and possibly in III, 181, XVI, 46. But *zabūr* is associated with David, IV, 161,

XVII, 57; XXI, 105 quotes Ps. xxxvii, 29 as being contained in *az-zabūr*.

But, as we have seen, the Qur'ān passed over into *al-kitāb*, 'the Book', which became the characteristic designation of the revelation. The idea of 'the Book' is important, but not quite easy to unravel. We must beware of reading back without question into the Qur'ān the developed Moslem doctrine of the heavenly Book, or eternal Qur'ān. The word *kitāb* is used in various senses. It occurs in the ordinary sense of 'something written', 'a letter', XXIV, 33, XXVII, 28 f. In connection with the Judgment it is used of a record of man's deeds, a kind of account such as we may suppose to have been known in Meccan business practice. Thus, each man is given his book, or writing, in his right or left hand, according as it shows a credit or a debit balance, XVII, 73, LXIX, 19, 25, LXXXIV, 7, 10. Or it is a record, a kind of ledger, kept by the angels who watch over the actions of men, LXXXII, 10 ff. At the Judgment-day the book will be produced, XVIII, 47, and the pages spread open, LXXXI, 10. In other passages, it is the book of God's knowledge, in which everything is recorded. "There is no secret thing in the heaven or the earth, but it is in a clear book", XXVII, 77. "There is no beast in the earth but Allah provides for it; He knoweth its lair and its resting-place; everything is in a clear book", XI, 8, cf. VI, 59, XXXIV, 3, etc. The dead remain in the book of Allah till the Day of Resurrection, XXX, 56. Or it is a record of God's decrees for what is to happen; "No misfortune has befallen the land or yourselves, but it was in a book before We brought it to be", LVII, 22. How far these uses were meant literally, or were figures of speech, it is impossible to say.

In any case, it is unlikely that the use of *kitāb* with reference to the revelation is derived from this idea of a book of God's knowledge embracing all things in heaven and earth, past, present and future, though in some Medinan passages it is a little difficult to distinguish between the two, cf. VIII, 76, IX, 36, XVII, 4, XXXIII, 6. To begin with, the reference is not to any heavenly book, but to the revelation which is in the hands of earlier monotheists. Confirmation of the truth of Muhammad's message is to be sought with those who have been given knowledge, XVII, 108, with the people of the Reminder, XVI, 45, XXI, 7, with those who recite the Book, X, 94, or with those who have knowledge of the Book, XIII, 43. The use of the term does indeed indicate more precisely the form in which they possess this revelation. It is a Book, perhaps commonly referred to as "the Book"; cf. the use of *hak-kāthūbh* among the Jews and *hē graphē* among Greek-speaking Christians. It is the authority for all religious belief and practice. Thus those who hold that the angels are female are asked to produce their Book, XXXV, 38, XXXVII, 157, XLIII, 20; and opponents are dismissed with the gibe that they "dispute about Allah without knowledge or guidance or light-giving Book", XXII, 8.

A divine source of this authoritative Book is no doubt implied, but the term itself evidently refers to the revelation as given to men. This is clear also in the often repeated statement that Moses was given the Book, VI, 155, XXIII, 51, etc.; or that he was given the guidance, and the Children of Israel inherited the Book, XL, 56. Occasionally Aaron is associated with him, XXV, 37, XXXVII, 114 ff., but usually it is Moses in particular to whom the Book was given as guidance for the Children of Israel. This, however, is not to be understood as limiting the possession of the Book to the Jews. It is not until we come to definitely Medinan passages that we find mention of Jews and Christians by their distinctive names, *Yahūd* and *Naṣārā*. It is only then that the existence of differences among monotheists became a problem to Muhammad. As Jesus was a messenger to the Children of Israel, the Christians were a branch of them. So also the designation, "People of the Book" applies, no doubt, mainly to the Jews of Medinah, with whom Muhammad was in direct relations, but that it, like "those who have been given the Book", which probably came earlier into use, includes the Christians also is shown by passages like III, 58 ff., IV, 169, V, 72. The Jews and Christians, in fact, both recite the Book, though they do not recognise each other's claims, II, 107. They "have made the Qur'ān bits", XV, 91, and "have cut their affair in pieces in the matter of Scriptures, each sect rejoicing in what is with them", XXIII, 55.

Thus we find reference to " those who have been given part of the Book ", III, 22, IV, 47, 54, the Jews being meant in each case. The Book of which Muhammad had been in quest thus turned out to be not one book but two, the Torah and the Evangel, terms also confined to Medinan passages. The Psalms given to David seem at this stage to be ignored. There were only two communities to whom the Book had previously been sent down, VI, 157, and the Torah and the Evangel were their Books. The Evangel is associated with Jesus. In two passages which belong to the period when he, like Muhammad himself, is represented as being sent to confirm what had previously been revealed, he is said to have been taught the Book and the Wisdom, the Torah and the Evangel, III, 43, V, 110; but later, when distinctions have hardened, he is said to have been given the Evangel, confirming the Torah, V, 50, LVII, 27. On the other hand, the Torah is never said to have been given to Moses. This may be mere accident, or it may be that the Torah, the distinctive Jewish Scripture, was regarded as associated with the differences which had arisen regarding the Book which had been given to Moses.

The realisation that there were more Books than one must have raised for Muhammad the question of their relation to the divine source. Even this problem, however, he resolved on the human level, by declaring that the differences had arisen after the revelation had been given, III, 17, XLI, 45, etc. The original revelation had thus been in essence the same. Whether it was conceived as having existed in the form of a heavenly Book is doubtful, but XLIII, 3: " Lo, it is in the mother of the Book in Our presence, exalted, wise " makes it probable that it was so, cf. XIII, 39. In any case, while the existence of other Books came to be recognised, the Book retains its original significance as an inclusive term for revelation in general, and to be given the Book is the mark of a prophet.

In Medinan times Muhammad's function as messenger is defined to be: " to recite the signs, to purify, and to teach the Book and the Wisdom ", II, 146, III, 158, LXII, 2. The

Wisdom, *al-ḥikmah*, thus associated with the Book or revealed truth, is, to judge by that given to Luqmān, XXXI, 11 ff., and to Muhammad himself, XVII, 41, the right conduct of life; it is a development of the ordinary sense of wisdom, particularly with regard to conduct. This is in line with the use of the cognate word *ḥukm* which clearly means the power of judging conduct or of laying down laws for the conduct of life. The verb *zakkā*, 'to purify', used for this part of the messenger's function, connects it with the *zakāt* either in the sense of voluntary alms, or, as it became in Medinah, the recognised levy whereby, according to Oriental conceptions, the possession of wealth was 'purified' by recognising God's right to a share of it. The 'signs' which are to be recited require some discussion.

The derivation of the word *'āyah*, 'sign', is doubtful.[1] It would most naturally be a native growth from a root corresponding to the Hebrew *'āwāh*, but such a root does not occur in Arabic. As a borrowing either from Hebrew *'ōth*, or from Syriac *'āthā*, the form is phonetically difficult to explain. But since the word was in use before Muhammad's time, its derivation is not so important for our purpose. In sense it corresponds to these Hebrew and Syriac words, and means a sign or indication of the presence of something else, and thus, a wonder or miracle as an indication of God's power or His intervention, or as an attestation of a message or messenger. We have seen that it is applied in the Qur'ān to the wonders of nature as attesting God's existence, His power and His bounty. One of the earliest functions of the messenger was to recite the 'signs' in that sense. But there are 'signs' also in the stories of former messengers, in the destruction of unbelieving peoples, XV, 75, etc., and in the deliverance of believers, XXIX, 23. There are 'signs' in the story of Joseph, XII, 7. The story of Mary and Jesus is a 'sign', XXI, 91. Some messengers had special 'signs' accorded them as confirmation of the truth of their message, as Ṣaliḥ, VII, 71, XI, 67, Jesus, III, 43, and in particular Moses, XX, 18 ff., XXVII, 12. When unbelievers demanded a 'sign' from Muhammad it was something of this sort that they wished,

[1] See p. 58.

VI, 37, XIII, 8, XXI, 5. Muhammad resisted the temptation to pose as a worker of miracles, but possibly this demand for a 'sign' had something to do with the shift of meaning in the word towards that of revelation. Muhammad's real 'signs' were the messages he received. Not only was there the mysterious way of 'suggestion' by which they came and which was the *bayyinah* or evidence of his claims, VI, 57, XI, 20, XLVII, 15. There were also the agreement of his teaching with what was in the Jewish Scriptures and the fact that the learned of the Children of Israel knew it, XX, 133, XXVI, 197. Moreover, previous revelation not only contained the record of many of the 'signs' and wonders which God had wrought, but was itself a very evident 'sign' of God's existence and interest in man.

Thus, the sense of the word *'āyāt* passes by scarcely definable gradations from that of 'signs' of God's existence, power and bounty shown in the wonders of nature, and of His interventions in human affairs shown in the wonder-stories of the past, to that of the religious truths and institutions revealed to previous messengers and to Muhammad himself. In late passages, it is his own deliverances which are primarily intended, but the word retains an indefiniteness of meaning which was no doubt useful and perhaps designed. Whether in the Qur'ān it ever came to mean 'verses' may be questioned. The strongest evidence is in passages like II, 100, XVI, 103, where there is reference to substituting one *'āyah* for another; but even there the sense may be not strictly a verse, but a separate deliverance. When, therefore, the 'signs' of the Qur'ān, or more frequently of the Book, are said to have been made distinct, *fuṣṣilat*, XLI, 2, it is doubtful if we can assume the phrase to refer to the insertion of rhyme-phrases at the end of verses. It may simply mean that the 'signs' have been set out one by one in separate deliverances. The word *bayyana*, on the other hand, often used in connection with the 'signs', seems to imply a restatement in clearer, more specific form, or the addition of some explanation. When the 'signs' are said to have been 'adjusted' (*aḥkama*), the sense is that they have been 'revised' or 'corrected', III, 5, XI, 1, XXII, 51.

From the above discussion it appears that during an important period of his religious activity Muhammad was concerned that his deliverances should correspond to the contents of earlier revelation. We may expect, then, that in the period extending from the time of his undertaking to produce a Qur'ān until he broke with the Jews of Medinah, the Qur'ān will show evidence of the influence of Scriptural ideas. As he seems, at any rate at first, to have had difficulty in finding out what the Scriptures contained, it will be interesting to see how these ideas take shape in the Qur'ān, and what parts of Scripture are reflected in it.

Eschatology.—To begin with, revelation was thought of as a doctrine of the Last Things, a message mainly of Judgment to come. This, as affecting the world in general, corresponds to the catastrophe which in the punishment-stories overtakes the particular unbelieving community. It, too, is *amr Allāh*, 'the affair of God', a phrase which, originally denoting God's intervention at the end of the story of a people or at the end of the world, is ultimately extended to include the whole process of God's intervention in the affairs of men; the sending of a prophet or messenger, the delivery of messages, the struggle with unbelief, and the establishment of the true religion.

There are a few passages in which there is merely a hint of evil effects following upon unbelief, for example XC, 1-11, XCII, 1-13, CIII, 1, 2, CIV, 1-4. The enigmatic verse XCV, 7 may perhaps indicate that Muhammad hesitated about proclaiming the Judgment, but it evidently came to him as a revealed truth which made a deep impression on his own mind, and may be ranked after the unity of God as the second great doctrine of Islam. Impressive pictures of the coming of the Last Judgment are characteristic of the early Qur'ān period.

These pictures are not, however, drawn for their own sake. With regard to the surroundings of the Last Judgment, Muhammad retains a genial freedom. His interest in them is that of the preacher, not that of one who tries to work out a complete picture, consistent in all its details. The main outlines of the doctrine are, however, clear enough. This world will come to an end. Men, restored to life, will come before God to be judged according to the deeds done in the body, and will be received into everlasting bliss, or cast into everlasting torment. This climax of world history is often referred to as *as-sā'ah*, 'the Hour'. The later standing term for it is *al-yawm al-ākhir*, 'the Last Day', or *yawm al-qiyāmah*, 'the Day of Resurrection'. Other terms used for it are *yawm ad-dīn*, 'the Day of Judgment', *yawm al-faṣl*, 'the Day of Distinction,' or separation of the good from the bad, *yawm al-jam'*, 'the Day of the Gathering' of men to the presence of God, *yawm at-talāqī*, 'the Day of Meeting' (with God).

The Hour comes suddenly, VI, 31, VII, 186, XII, 107, XXII, 54, XLIII, 66, XLVII, 20. It is heralded by a shout, *ṣaiḥah*, XXXVI, 53, by a thunderclap, *ṣākhkhah*, LXXX, 33, or by the sound of a trumpet, LXIX, 13, LXXVIII, 18, (in XXXIX, 68, two blasts are referred to, each heralding a distinct stage). A cosmic upheaval takes place. The mountains dissolve into dust, the seas boil up, the sun is darkened, the stars fall, the sky is rolled up. The graves are opened and human beings of all ages hurry in crowds to appear before the Judge. The presence of the Judge is hinted at rather than described ; in XXXIX, 75 the angels are seen circling the throne about, in LXXXIX, 23 Allah comes with the angels, rank upon rank ; cf. LXXVIII, 38.

The similarity of all this to Jewish and Christian ideas is evident and need not here be followed out in detail.[1] Most of the details can be traced back to Scripture, though occasionally an original trait is added to adapt the picture to Arab conditions, as in LXXXI, 4. It was, however, in Apocalyptic literature that these ideas were most freely developed, and, as that literature was in the centuries immediately preceding Islam cultivated in the Christian Church rather than in Judaism, the presumption is that Muhammad was, at this stage, in touch with Christians rather than with Jews. But the Qur'ān-pictures do not follow the lines of any one description of the Last Day to which we can point.

[1] See Andrae, *Der Ursprung des Islams und das Christentum*, p. 59 ff., and Ahrens, *Z.D.M.G.*, 1930.

The impression we get is rather that items of popular belief have been absorbed, passed through the Prophet's own reflection, and used for his immediate purposes.

It may be pointed out here that the Qur'ān doctrine of resurrection does not imply the natural immortality of the human soul. Man's existence is entirely dependent upon Allah's will; when He wills He causes him to die; when He wills He calls him to life again. To the scoffing objection of the Meccans that former generations had been dead a long time and their bodies had mouldered to dust and rotten bones, the reply is simply that God is none the less able to restore them to life, and that they will then have no knowledge of the length of time that has elapsed. Some Medinan passages, however, imply that the soul has a continuous existence apart from the body, that judgment upon it takes place immediately after death, and that those who have died for the cause of Allah are already in felicity, II, 149, III, 163 ff.

With regard to the actual Judgment, the Qur'ān descriptions are much more original. The books will be opened, and a man's account will be handed to him and he will be asked to read it. That might be a borrowed idea, or it might be an adaptation of the business practice of Meccah. The trait that the good will receive their account in their right hands, while the bad receive theirs in their left, is thought by Rudolph to have been suggested by some Christian picture which Muhammad may have seen—an interesting possibility but nothing more. It might be based upon the Judgment-scene in the Gospel of Matthew xxv, 31 ff., which other evidence suggests was known to Muhammad. But there are many dramatic Judgment-scenes which quite evidently arise out of the situation in which Muhammad found himself with his opponents—a free using of the Judgment idea to enforce his doctrines.

The criterion by which men are judged is prevailingly belief or unbelief. But good and evil deeds enter into the account. In fact, in spite of the prominence which belief assumes, the ground of judgment is fundamentally moral, not intellectual. Belief, the acceptance of the messenger and his message, was to Muhammad a moral act, and was the gateway to real uprightness of life and conduct. When he is brought up against the claim of Jews, or of Christians, to acceptance with God on the ground of their faith, and their denial of acceptance to those of other faiths, he falls back upon the moral ground of judgment. " It is not by your dogmas or the dogmas of the People of the Book ; whoever does evil will be requited for it, and will not find for himself, apart from Allah, either patron or helper. But whoever does works of righteousness, be it male or female, and is a believer —they will enter the Garden and will not be wronged a speck ", IV, 122 f. Hence the Judgment is sometimes spoken of as a balance in which good and bad deeds of men are weighed : " As for him whose balances are heavy, he shall be in life satisfactory, but as for him whose balances are light, he shall perish ", CI, 5, 6.

The result of the Judgment is either everlasting bliss or everlasting torment. There is no middle place. One passage, VII, 44, has sometimes been taken as implying a middle state, but this probably rests on a misinterpretation. Another passage says that all shall go down to it (that is, hell-fire), and that then those who have shown piety will be delivered from it, XIX, 72 f. That might be taken to imply a kind of purgatory for believers, from which they will pass to their reward after being purified from the evil they may have committed. But probably the sense is not that, but rather that all men will be brought face to face with the pains of hell, from which, however, those who have shown piety will as the result of the Judgment be exempted. True, there are grades, at least in heaven. Some are brought nearer to God than others, and in one passage at least, LVI, 87 ff., we seem to have three classes ; those who are brought near, those of the right hand, who are blessed, and those of the left hand, who are consigned to hell. Who " those brought near " are, is not clear ; possibly it refers to the prophets and special servants of Allah in this life.

Descriptions of the future life come late in the Qur'ān-period. The abode of the wicked who are condemned at the Judgment is *jahannam*. Other names applied to it are *al-jaḥīm*, ' the Hot Place ', *saqar* (a word of uncertain meaning and origin), *sa'īr*, 'blaze', *laẓā* (LXX, 15), probably not a proper name but simply 'a blaze'. Most common of all perhaps, especially in later passages, is *an-nār*, 'the Fire'. The torments of the damned therein are depicted with a great wealth of imagery. The main idea remains constant, but the details it is probably impossible to bring into a consistent picture. Evidently the idea is Christian, possibly Jewish but more probably Christian, in spite of the ultimate derivation of *jahannam*, perhaps through Ethiopic from the Hebrew *gē-hinnōm*. But Muhammad used it quite freely, adapting it to his own uses and circumstances. No doubt many of the details could be paralleled in Christian literature, and Andrae has found parallels for a number, for example, the idea of the overseers of hell and those who administer punishment to the condemned souls being angels, that is, good beings commissioned by Allah so to do; and the idea that the inmates of hell will ask the inmates of Paradise for water, VII, 48. That is fairly late and is an evident reminiscence of the parable of Lazarus in the Gospel. So also the chains and fetters with which the wicked are bound are perhaps suggested by the chain with which Satan is bound in the Apocalypse of John. On the other hand, the tree of *zaqqūm* from which the damned shall eat is an Arabian touch—this tree, said to have been one which grew in the Ḥijāz, had a very bitter fruit; probably an Arabian touch too is that they will be given hot water to drink. Altogether, we have the impression of an original mind using suggestions which came to hand in order to embellish the central idea and stamp the terrors of future punishment upon hard and scoffing hearts.

The common designation for the abode of the Just is *al-jannah*, 'the Garden', often 'a Garden, through which the rivers flow'. This is no doubt the Garden of Eden. In fact we find it designated *jannat 'adn*, or by translation of the latter word regarded as Arabic, *jannat an-na'īm*, or simply *an-na'īm*. In some late passages we find *firdaws*, a singular produced from *farādīs*, the Greek *paradeisos*. Usually the Garden is spoken of in the singular, but in LV, 46 we find the dual used—as some people think because of the exigencies of rhyme; four gardens indeed are mentioned in that surah, for beside the first two are other two (v. 62). Wellhausen regards this latter part of the surah as simply a duplicate of the former, but I incline to think that the four gardens arise from an early misunderstanding of the four rivers of Paradise mentioned in Genesis. In the Garden the blessed enjoy luxuries, they recline on couches, they eat fruit, they drink wine which is served to them by heavenly ever-youthful boys. (This last detail Horovitz thinks is derived from the banquets of Arab chiefs at which boys served.) Wine, of course, occurs in Christian descriptions of the joys of heaven. What is noticeable is that Muhammad cannot, at first, have had the antipathy to wine which afterwards led him to forbid its use altogether. There are also ever-flowing springs in Paradise, and there are milk and honey. Again, Christian literature provides parallels for most of these details and for the more spiritual elements in the reward of the pious, which are by no means absent, for example, forgiveness, peace, and the satisfaction of the soul in God. But the use of these material things is individual. There are features derived from the experience of Muhammad and his followers, such as the absence of gossip and babble, that is, escape from the jeering ridicule with which they were surrounded in Meccah.

The most mysterious element in the Qur'ān conception of Paradise is that of the Ḥūrīs, the beautiful, chaste, purified female companions of the blessed. The word properly means 'white' or 'bright-eyed', and is often accompanied by the word *'īn*, 'having eyes' or 'wide-eyed'. They are pictured as modest, retiring, restraining their glances, and as being enclosed in pavilions like treasured pearls. Whether the same idea is contained in the "purified spouses" of the Medinan passages, II, 23, III, 13, IV, 60, is not quite certain, but is possible. That would support the suggestion that they are simply the sublimation of the earthly relationship of the sexes, but, as the descriptions of them occur in earlier passages where the background of Christian eschatology is otherwise very evident, this is not very likely. The suggestion for them has been found in Zoroastrianism, where the idea sometimes occurs that the virtues which a man has acquired in life bear him company in the life to come as angelic beings. It is doubtful, however, whether this imaginative conception is to be found in Zoroastrianism early enough to have affected the Qur'ān. Wensinck suggests that we have again an idea suggested by the sight of Christian pictures of angelic beings associating with the redeemed in Paradise. As to the pictures, I should be doubtful, but probably we have here some reflection of Christian conceptions of angels in Paradise.

NARRATIVES

It is in the narrative portions of the Qur'ān that its dependence upon the Bible, especially upon the Old Testament, is most evident. Some of the punishment-stories, those of 'Ād, Thamūd and Sheba, and probably the references to the peoples of ar-Rass and al-Aikah are derived from Arab sources. It may be, too, that some vague knowledge of the stories of Noah, Lot and Pharaoh was current in Arabia, but the great bulk of the material which Muhammad used to illustrate and enforce his teaching was derived from Jewish and Christian sources, and was meant to reproduce what was contained in the revelation given to the People of the Book.

The creation of the heavens and the earth in six days is frequently referred to; the creation, temptation and fall of Adam are recounted in VII, 10 ff., XX, 115 ff. There is a version of the story of Cain and Abel in V, 30 ff. The story of Noah appears among the punishment-stories; it is later transformed into a prophetic story, though the surah devoted to him, LXXI, is based largely on Muhammad's own experience. Lot also is the centre of a punishment-story but appears amongst other Biblical personages in XXI, 74 f. as endowed with jurisdiction and knowledge. Abraham appears in the prelude to the Lot-story, then becomes himself the centre of a punishment-story; finally in Medinah he becomes a prophet, the founder of the Arab religion. Ishmael is mentioned separately, but is ultimately associated with Abraham in establishing the Kaʿbah. In spite of his importance, however, as the link between Abraham and the Arabs, little information is given about him. That, as Moslems hold, it was he whom Abraham was commanded to sacrifice, XXXVII, 100 ff., is by no means certain. Isaac and Jacob are mentioned in connection with Abraham, but little is told of them. A whole surah, XII, is devoted to the story of Joseph. Moses was naturally of great interest to Muhammad as a previous messenger, and as having been the recipient of the Book. Besides many references, there are several versions of his story, LXXIX, 15 ff., XX, 8 ff., XXVII, 7 ff., XXVI, 9 ff., XXVIII, 2 ff., VII, 101 ff., which, when analysed, show growing acquaintance with the Biblical narrative. In sum, the story includes Moses' birth, his upbringing in Pharaoh's household, his killing of the Egyptian and flight to Midian, his call and mission to Pharaoh, the association of Aaron with him, his contest with the magicians, the plagues, the deliverance of the Children of Israel, the drowning of Pharaoh's hosts in the sea, the giving of the Law, the worship of the Golden Calf, and the main incidents of the desert wanderings including the refusal of the Children of Israel to enter the Promised Land. That as-Sāmirī, who appears in XX in connection with the Golden Calf, is a reminiscence of Jeroboam " who made Israel to sin " by setting up calf-worship in Samaria, is probable but not certain. References to the historical books of the Old Testament are relatively few. Saul (Ṭālūt) appears in contest with Goliath (Jālūt), who, however, is killed by David, II, 248 ff. To David were given the Psalms; by some confusion he is also referred to as a maker of coats of mail, XXXIV, 10. There is a reminiscence of Nathan's parable in XXXVIII, 20 ff. Solomon is a great builder, a lover of horses, and master of winds and jinn, XXXIV, 11 ff., XXXVIII, 29 ff. A lengthy account of his meeting with the Queen of Sheba is given in XXVII, 15 ff. A reminiscence of Elijah's contest with the priests of Baal appears in XXXVII, 123 ff. The story of Jonah is briefly summarised in the same surah. Elisha is, no doubt, Alyasaʿ who is mentioned in VI, 86 and XXXVIII, 48; but nothing is told of him, unless we see two short notes connected with him embedded in the story of Job in XXXVIII, 40 ff. What is told of Job comes from the framework story. Haman is mentioned, but transferred to the time of Pharaoh. Idrīs, whom Noeldeke identified with Andreas, is more probably Esdras, as suggested by Torrey. Ezra appears also as 'Uzair in IX, 30. Who is meant by Dhū l-Kifl, XXI, 85, XXXVIII, 48, is quite uncertain.[1]

The New Testament contributes much less narrative material than the Old. The story of Zecharias and the birth of John (Yaḥyā), XIX, 1 ff. might come from the Gospel of Luke, but that of the Annunciation and the birth of Jesus which follows, cf. also III, 30 ff., shows the influence of Apocryphal gospels, particularly that of James. So also does the account of Jesus as a messenger to the Children of Israel, III, 43, V, 109 f. The reference to the Crucifixion, IV, 156 f., may show Docetic influence. There is a reminiscence of the parable of the wise and foolish virgins in LVII, 13 f., and some influence of the parable of Dives and Lazarus, and of the Judgment-scene in Luke xvi, 19 ff., appears in VII, 48 f. The account of the institution of the Lord's Supper, V, 112 ff., obviously does not go back to literary sources, but is based on some meagre answer to an enquiry regarding the origin of the rite.

Examination of these parallels to Biblical narratives shows that they were not taken directly from the Bible. It must, of course, be remembered, that Muhammad was never simply a borrower. Material which came to him from outside sources was always made his own, moulded by reflection, and freely used for his own purposes. There is, for instance, an evident tendency to formalise these Biblical stories and group them together by refrains, as had been done with the punishment-stories; this is specially evident in XXXVII, but appears also elsewhere. Allowance being made for this, it is still clear that the material did not come to him from literary sources. There are strange discrepancies and omissions in the narratives. An incident from the story of Gideon

[1] See my article on "Muhammad's Knowledge of the Old Testament" in *Studia Semitica et Orientalia*, II, Glasgow, 1945.

appears in the account of Saul, II, 250, and a reminiscence of the story of Jacob affects the story of Moses, XXVIII, 27. Mary the mother of Jesus is confused with Miriam the sister of Moses, XIX, 29. Further, practically all these narratives have an admixture of Talmudic or other extra-Biblical material, or show traits which can be explained only by statements which occur in Jewish or Christian tradition. Such statements or allusions, however troublesome to modern scholars, may well have haunted the memory of Muhammad's contemporaries who had any knowledge of religious matters. In fact, the whole choice of material is such as to suggest that it came from the memories of men and was communicated to him orally.

The haphazard lists of names, as in VI, XIX, XXI, XXXVII and XXXVIII, the partial way in which the stories of the persons are filled in, and the difficulty evidently experienced in getting the persons into historical order and connection, all argue against his having received any systematic instruction; they point rather to his having made enquiries of people who happened to be available and were likely to have information to give. The forms of some of the names, for example *Ilyās* (Elias) for Elijah, *Yūnus* for Jonah, seem to indicate that some even of the Old Testament material came to him through Christian channels. From the presence of so much Talmudic material it may be confidently inferred that he was in touch with Jews also, as we know he was in Medinah, and probably towards the end of his Meccan period as well.

The supposition that Muhammad was dependent upon 'lay' informants whose memories were not always clear as to what was actually in Scripture explains also the presence in the Qur'ān of extra-Biblical stories and of material which does not strictly belong to religious literature at all. Not only do we find the story of the fall of Iblīs from among the angels of heaven conjoined with the story of the creation and of the fall of Adam, but we find also in XVIII the legend of the Seven Sleepers, and the curious story of Moses and al-Khidr, and a story of Dhū l-Qarnain, that is, Alexander the Great. The legend of the Seven Sleepers, like the

Romance of Alexander, from which the other two stories are derived, was no doubt widespread in the Christian East. To Muhammad, enquiring as to the revelation given to previous monotheists, these stories may well have been recounted ; they were part of the thought-world of the countries round about Arabia.

In Medinah Muhammad was in a better position to learn the actual contents of, at any rate, the Old Testament, than he had been in Meccah, for he was in contact with colonies of Jews who had, no doubt, amongst them scholars and rabbis. There are some indications that he made use of these opportunities and acquired a fairly good knowledge of, at least, the Books of Moses. He found that food-laws belonged to the time of Moses, and had not existed before that. And he made the momentous discovery that Abraham had lived before the time of Moses, and was therefore neither Jew nor Christian, but an independent recipient of God's favour, III, 58 ff. That this was new to him is shown by the resentful accusation that the Jews had concealed what was in Scripture. It is significant also that some of the revisions to be discerned in the surahs seem designed to remove non-Biblical material which had been used, II, 95 ff., XI, 43 ff.

Of the New Testament Muhammad seems never to have acquired any intimate knowledge. The Gospel parables, one feels, would have appealed to him had he known them, but few of them find any echo in the Qur'ān. The reason probably is that he was never brought into such close relations with Christians as he was with the Jews in Medinah. His quarrel with the latter led to his turning away from the People of the Book, so that he was no longer concerned to reproduce what the Book contained. Christians too, he discovered, were as little open to recognise his claims as the Jews had been, II, 105. Their doctrines of the divine Sonship of Christ and of the Trinity seemed to him, as he understood them on apparently very imperfect information, to contradict his fundamental dogma of the unity of God. Thus he was repelled, and in the end became hostile.

LEGISLATION

The legal portions of the Qur'ān are mostly of Medinan date, and are closely related to Muhammad's policy during that period. To set them in their historical context belongs rather to a biography of the Prophet than to an introduction to the Qur'ān. Only the main subjects can be here indicated.

Prayer.—The *ṣalāt* was introduced in Meccah, but at what point in the Meccan period is difficult to determine. As the word is Syriac, it probably belongs to the approximation to Christian practice and ideas which took place in the middle of that period and led to the beginning of the special Qur'ān. The practice of night-vigils, which was for a time recommended, though afterwards moderated, confirms its Christian origin. No regulations are prescribed as to the conduct of the *ṣalāt*. It is a little doubtful whether the five daily prayers are actually laid down in the Qur'ān. In Meccan passages the usual prescription is morning and evening prayer, with the additional recommendation of some part of the night being spent in prayer and recitation. A "middle prayer" was ordained in Medinah. The other two legal times depend upon revision and combination of passages, and may not have been intended. The direction of prayer towards Jerusalem was part of the approach to the Jews at the time of the Hijrah, as the change to Meccah was a sign of the break with them.

Poor-Tax.—The word *zakāt* is Syriac and therefore Christian. It and the related verb occur in Meccan passages, but only in the sense of alms and voluntary giving to the poor, as much for the purification of the giver's soul as for relief of the needy. The institution of *zakāt* as a duty incumbent upon Moslems grew out of this and is nowhere regulated. Its beginning belongs to the first year or two in Medinah, and was motived by the circumstances of the poorer Muhājirīn and necessities of state.

Food.—This was one of the first subjects which proximity to the Jews brought to notice in Medinah. There were no food-laws in Muhammad's early teaching. Several Meccan portions of the Qur'ān are directed against pagan food-taboos, and characterise as ingratitude the refusal to use the good things which Allah provides. What were "good things" was no doubt left to Arab custom and convention to determine. The Jews, however, had their elaborate regulations as to clean and unclean animals, which must have been irksome to Arab taste. In the endeavour to approximate to them in Medinah, it was at first laid down that food allowable for those who had been given the Book was allowable for Muhammad's followers, V, 7. Later, as his quarrel with the Jews increased, their food-laws were regarded as a punishment laid upon them for their rebelliousness. His followers, however, seem to have pressed for guidance in the matter, and rules were laid down which correspond pretty much to what was laid down for Christians by the Council of Jerusalem, Acts, xv, 29. The main point of difference is the prohibition of the use of swine-flesh.

Drink.—The Qur'ān prohibits wine, *khamr*, V, 92. It was probably practical reasons which led to this prohibition, though *khamr* denotes wine made from grapes, which was not native to Arabia and the trade in which was largely in the hands of Jews and Christians. But Muhammad had disagreeable experiences with followers who had indulged in it, and found it necessary to reprimand some who came to prayer in a state of intoxication, IV, 46. So wine, which had been mentioned as one of the delights of Paradise, XLVII, 16, came to be disapproved of for its evil effects, II, 216, and finally forbidden altogether.

Gambling.—This was represented in Arabia by the game of *maisir*, which is conjoined with wine in II, 216, and V, 92. The latter passage also forbids the use of divining arrows, the Arab form of drawing or casting lots.

Fasting.—This does not appear in the Prophet's Meccan teaching. Its introduction is part of the assimilation to the People of the Book at the beginning of the Medinan period. The adoption of the Jewish fast of the 'Āshūrā, which, Tradition attests, is probably laid down in II, 179, 180. The following verse substitutes for this the month of Ramaḍān as the period of the fast. Some influence of the Christian

Lent may have contributed to the choice of this extended period. But the lunar month was, to the Arabs, an important division of time. The selection of Ramaḍān is probably due to the battle of Badr having been fought and won in that month. This is difficult to reconcile with the statements of Tradition, but of course Tradition does not recognise that v. 181 is later than v. 180. The regulations of v. 183, which allow marital intercourse and eating and drinking during the night, belong to a still later time.

Pilgrimage.—This was a pre-Islamic practice, though it seems to have been connected with places in the neighbourhood rather than with Meccah itself. It was probably recognised early as part of the religion of Abraham, II, 192 ff., XXII, 27 ff. The bloodshed at Badr, however, made it extremely dangerous for any Moslem to visit Meccah ; so the ʻĪd al-aḍḥā (Bairām) was instituted, and the animals which would otherwise have been sent to Meccah to be sacrificed at the close of the pilgrimage were permitted to be sacrificed at home. The treaty of Ḥudaibiyah stipulated for a Moslem visit to the Kaʻbah the following year, cf. XLVIII, 27. On the conquest of Meccah the Kaʻbah was cleansed of idols, and by the proclamation made shortly afterwards polytheists were forbidden to approach it, IX, 28. Tradition says that they were debarred from the pilgrimage itself by a proclamation read by ʻAlī a year later. But the final regulation of the pilgrimage belongs to Muhammad's farewell visit, and is not contained in the Qur'ān.

Usury.—The taking of interest was no doubt a common practice in Meccah. The disapproval of it in the Qur'ān, however, belongs to the Medinan period, and may be connected with the revulsion from the Jews, who are accused of disobeying their own law, rather than from the Meccans. The putting of money out to interest is unfavourably contrasted with giving it as *zakāt*, XXX, 38. It is forbidden to believers, III, 125, and sternly disapproved of, II, 276; accrued interest is ordered to be abandoned, II, 278.

Marriage.—As part of the friendly approach to the People of the Book in early-Medinan days, the list of forbidden degrees of kinship in marriage was taken over from the Jews, with modifications to include milk-kinship, which was important in Arab sentiment, IV, 27, 31; cf. Leviticus xviii, 6 ff. It is allowable to marry women of the People of the Book, V, 7, but marriage with idolaters is forbidden, II, 220. Polygamy is allowed. The express permission to take wives up to four in number, IV, 3, was probably occasioned by the circumstances after the battle of Uḥud; many Moslems had been killed and their widows and orphans had to be provided for. They must, however, be treated fairly, as far as is humanly possible, IV, 3, 128. It is also permissible to marry slaves, and slave concubines are allowed, IV, 29, XXIII, 6. Whether the *mutʿah*, or temporary marriage, is permitted by IV, 28, is a moot point; the verse certainly represents a liberal concession to Arab laxity.

Divorce.—In this also Arab custom was lax. Muhammad aimed at restraining this licence, but was only partially successful. The legislation of II, 228 ff. left the right of divorce in the hands of the man, but was intended to secure adequate time for reflection and fair treatment of the woman if divorce should be ultimately resolved upon. A three-months' waiting-time was prescribed, in which reconciliation might be effected and the marriage be reconstituted without divorce having actually taken place. If, however, the parties were so ill-assorted that this happened three times, it was better that divorce should take place, and should be final, the woman being free to become the wife of another man. This was probably borrowed from Jewish law or practice. Moslem law has, however, regarded the three-months' waiting-time as applying only to the woman; divorce takes place at once, but the woman may be taken back if the husband relents. If, however, divorce takes place three times, he cannot take her back unless she has meanwhile remarried and been divorced. This has led to abuses which were certainly not intended.

Inheritance.—Several passages deal with this subject, but the rules laid down are by no means easy to systematise. It was probably customary amongst the Arabs, or at any rate the Meccans, to give instructions before death as to the disposal of their property, XXXVI, 50. But the form of

II, 176 ff., laying this down as a duty for believers, seems to imply that it was regarded as Scriptural and probably intended to conform to Jewish practice. These instructions are to be witnessed, but it is not said that they should be written. Further rules as to witnesses are given in V, 105 ff., which is much later in date. The detailed rules of IV, 12 ff. seem naturally to refer to the division of the residue of an estate, but this is disputed by the legalists. They show no trace of Jewish influence, and probably represent a reform of Arab practice. The shares of children, parents, and, in the case of there being no direct heirs, brothers and sisters, are laid down. No special privilege is given to the first-born. Females inherit along with males, though, as a general principle, the male receives the portion of two females. The right of women to hold property is thus recognised. No share is here assigned to a widow, though a husband's share in a wife's property is specified. To make provision for a widow was, however, laid down as a duty, II, 241 ; cf. IV. 37.

Other subjects which are dealt with need not be specially treated here. During most of the Medinan period the Prophet and his followers were involved in fighting, and war against unbelievers is urged in various passages. The division of spoil is regulated. Slavery is accepted as an institution, but slaves are to be kindly treated, IV, 40, and the liberation of a slave is regarded as meritorious. Contracts are to be kept, V, 1, debts are to be recorded, II, 282, and theft is to be punished by cutting off the hand, V, 42. Adultery also is to be severely punished, but is made difficult to prove by the demand for four witnesses, XXIV, 13. Conduct in public audiences and private interviews with the Prophet is referred to, and even private matters of the harem are not excluded. Qur'ān legislation is, in fact, the record of how the many and varied problems which beset Muhammad as head of the new militant religious community of Islam were dealt with. It is a testimony to both the variety of his experience and the soundness of his mind that later jurists were able to make it the basis of a complete system of law which has not yet altogether lost its validity.

CONCLUSION

In addition to the specially doctrinal, narrative and legal passages, the Qur'ān contains many others; addresses, exhortations to his followers, public documents, as in IX, 1 ff., and private reflections which throw light upon the character of Muhammad and the methods by which he guided and ruled the infant community which his religious teaching had called into being. The book, especially in its Medinan portions, is the mirror of a varied and eventful career. It shows us a man of great natural ability, shrewdness and foresight, essentially reserved and withdrawn, following the promptings which came to him in times of privacy and reflection, yet sensitive to the moods, feelings and thoughts of those about him. Himself an Arab, he began his work in an Arab environment, modified in Meccah by trade and new-made wealth. The thought-world of Arabia had probably been affected by the presence of Jewish colonies, and included at least some superficial knowledge of Christianity, especially on the part of those who had visited any of the neighbouring countries. It was not, however, until faced by the failure of his general mission and the necessity of providing a ritual of worship for his small band of followers, that he set himself to acquire a knowledge of the revelation which had been given to the People of the Book, in order to communicate it to his own people. As he seems to have been dependent on chance informants, the parallels of the Qur'ān with the contents of Scripture often show discrepancies, omissions, and inclusion of outside matter. At first his informants seem to have been Christians but later the Old Testament material is strongly coloured by Jewish tradition, largely oral. In Medinah, as we know, he was in close contact with Jews, and at the beginning of that period Jewish influence upon the Qur'ān is strong. Shaking himself free of the People of the Book, who had proved hostile, he became by way of the religion of Abraham the independent teacher and prophet whose aim was no longer to convey to the Arabs what the People of the Book held as revealed religion, but so to transform Arab custom as to suit monotheistic belief. Indirectly the influence of Judaism and Christianity still remained. Of the former he had gained a fairly intimate knowledge; of the latter the same cannot be said. The conceptions of some cardinal Christian doctrines reflected in the Qur'ān and the entire omission of others show that he had never been in contact with theologically educated Christians, but depended on popular accounts. How far less obvious influences coloured his environment and his sources of information is difficult to determine. Mandaean, Manichaean, Persian and other influences have been suggested, but have not been convincingly proved. It is not always easy to distinguish between the material which Muhammad may have received and the form which he himself may have given it in reproducing it. For, in dealing with the sources of the Qur'ān, we must never forget that the main source, after all, is the brooding mind of the Prophet himself, enlightened, as he believed, by the divine guidance which came to him through reflection and meditation.

WORDS IN THE QUR'AN WHOSE DERIVATION OR MEANING IS DISCUSSED

(The numbers refer to pages)

BIBLIOGRAPHY

Ahrens, K. Muhammed als Religionsstifter. Leipzig, 1935.
Andrae, Tor. Der Ursprung des Islams und das Christentum. Upsala, 1926.
  Muhammad, the Man and his Faith. Translated into English by Th. Menzel, London, 1936.
al-Bai ḍāwī. Anwār at-Tanzīl. Cairo, 1330.
Bell, R. The Origin of Islam in its Christian Environment. London, 1926.
  The Qur'ān. Translated, with a Critical Re-arrangement of the Surahs. Edinburgh, 1937–39.
Blachère, R. Le Coran. Paris, 1947–51.
al-Bukhārī. Al-Jāmi'aṣ-Ṣaḥīḥ. Leyden, 1862–1908.
Casanova, P. Mohammed et la fin du monde. Paris, 1911–24.
Geiger, A. Was hat Mohammed aus dem Judenthume aufgenommen? Bonn, 1833.

Grimme, H. Mohammed. Münster, 1892–95.
Hirschfeld, H. New Researches into the Composition and Exegesis of the Qur'ān. London, 1902.
Horowitz, J. Das koranische Paradies (*in* Scripta Universitatis atque Bibliothecae Hierosolymitarum). Jerusalem, 1923.
Koranische Untersuchungen. Berlin, 1926.
Ibn Hishām. Sīrat an-Nabīy. Cairo, 1329.
Ibn Manzūr. Lisān al-'Arab. Cairo, 1308.
Jeffery, A. Materials for the History of the Text of the Qur'ān. Leyden, 1937.
The Foreign Vocabulary of the Qur'ān. Baroda, 1938.
Margoliouth, D. S. Mohammed and the Rise of Islam. New York and London, 1905.
Mohammed. London and Glasgow, 1939.
Mingana, A. Woodbrooke Studies. Cambridge, 1928.
Mueller, D. H. Die Propheten in ihrer ursprünglichen Form. Vienna, 1895.
Muir, Sir W. Life of Mohammad. Revised Edition by T. H. Weir, Edinburgh, 1928.
Noeldeke, Th. Geschichte des Korans. Göttingen, 1860.
Geschichte des Korans. 2nd Edition by Schwally and others, Leipzig, 1909–19.
Neue Beiträge zur semitischen Sprachwissenschaft. Strassburg, 1910.
Rodwell, J. M. Translation of the Qur'ān. London, 1876.
Rudolph, W. Die Abhängigkeit des Korans von Judenthum und Christenthum. Stuttgart, 1922.
Sabbagh, T. La Métaphore dans le Coran. Paris, 1943.
Sprenger, A. Das Leben und die Lehre des Mohammad. Berlin, 1861–65.
as-Suyūṭī. Al-Itqān fī'Ulūm al-Qur'ān. Calcutta, 1852–54.
Torrey, C. C. The Commercial-Theological Terms in the Koran. Leyden, 1892.
The Jewish Foundation of Islam. New York, 1933.
Vollers, K. Volkssprache und Schriftsprache im alten Arabien. Strassburg, 1906.
Weil, G. Historisch-kritische Einleitung in den Koran. 2nd Edition, Bielefeld, 1878.
Wellhausen, J. The Arab Kingdom and its Fall. Translated into English by M. G. Weir, Calcutta, 1927.
Wensinck, A. J. Mohammed en de Joden te Medina. Leyden, 1908.
The Muslim Creed. Cambridge, 1932.

Journals:
Der Islam.
Göttinger Gelehrte Anzeigen.
Journal of the Royal Asiatic Society (J.R.A.S.).
Studia Semitica et Orientalia.
The Moslem World.
Zeitschrift der deutschen Morgenländischen Gesellschaft (Z.D.M.G.).

INDEX OF REFERENCES TO THE QUR'AN

References to the columns of surahs on pp. ix-x, 63-66, and 110-113 are not included.
I, II, etc., indicate the surahs.
'General' indicates a reference to part or whole of the surah.

SELECT INDEX

The Table of Contents should also be consulted
(The numbers refer to pages)